THE DELINQUENT AND NON-DELINQUENT IN A HIGH DELINQUENT AREA

LAWRENCE ROSEN

San Francisco, California
1978

Published by

R AND E RESEARCH ASSOCIATES
4843 Mission Street, San Francisco 94112

Publishers

Robert D. Reed and Adam S. Eterovich

Library of Congress Card Catalog Number

77-91431

ISBN

0-88247-520-7

TABLE OF CONTENTS

ACKNOWLEDGMENTS

There are several persons who have been of assistance in this endeavor, and to whom I am most appreciative. They include Leonard Savitz, Robert Bell, Roscoe Hinkle and Robert West. To my former mentor, Michael Lalli and former colleague, Stanley Turner, I owe my gratitude as well, for the many valuable discussions on topics related to this study.

There are several personages outside of Temple to whom I am grateful: Al Toisser, Philadelphia City Planning Commission for use of and assistance with the Philadelphia Real Estate Directory; Winifred A. Grant, Eleanor Laws and Helena Sykes, Department of Records, City of Philadelphia, for their assistance and patience in the many long hours of searching property deeds.

I also wish to acknowledge Temple University Computing Center for use of the IBM 1401 computer and to the general assistance of the Sociology Department at Temple.

And finally, to my wife Sonja for her many long, and seemingly endless, hours of typing.

CHAPTER ONE

INTRODUCTION

Ever since the publication of the pioneering work of <u>Delinquency Areas</u>,[1]
it has been widely accepted that certain areas of large cities have a dispro-
portionate amount of delinquents. Numerous ecological studies have attempted
to find the variables which would account for the spatial distribution of delinquents,[2] and this research has demonstrated a fairly high correlation of
many independent variables with delinquent rates.

On the basis of these findings there may be a tendency to assert that the
variables found to be ecologically important would also prove important for individual delinquency. In other words, if a variable exhibits a high ecological
correlation with delinquent rates, then youths possessing that variable (or
absence of it, if the correlation is negative) would have a greater probability
of being delinquent. A corollary to this idea is that it would be possible to
distinguish between the delinquent and the non-delinquent in a high delinquent
area by simply having knowledge of the variable. Of course, it is widely known
that this is not necessarily true; it could be true, but this has to be demonstrated. This is what W. S. Robinson meant when he asserted that ecological
correlations should not be used uncritically to make inferences about individuals.[3] (No criticism of ecological correlations is intended here because inference to individual behavior from ecological correlations is not always possible. Certainly, ecological correlations are a legitimate enterprise in their
own right.[4] In addition, it is possible, under certain assumptions, to make
inferences about individuals from ecological data.[5] The only criticism intended
is of those who misuse ecological correlations.)

The primary purpose of this study is to determine if several of the variables proven successful in the ecological analysis of delinquents will be successful as well in distinguishing between delinquents and non-delinquents in a
high delinquent area.[6] It is <u>not</u> the intention of this study to investigate
the more general problem of determining if the same variables which are ecologically important would be important for individuals in general. This was impossible to do on a systematic basis because: (1) several variables employed
in ecological studies were not included in the design of the larger project
from which this study is drawn (e.g., family income and quality of housing);
(2) some ecological variables are difficult to assign to individuals (e.g., number of commercial establishments and persons per square mile); (3) the necessary
research design of using a low delinquent area as well as a high delinquent area
could not be utilized because a low delinquent area was not included in the design of the larger project from which the data for the present study was taken.
This type of design is necessary in order to determine if the independent variables in question have a general effect for youths, independent of residence,
or a special effect for either a low or high delinquent area. Despite this inability to investigate the more general problem, an analysis of individual delinquents in a high delinquent area is still of great importance for several reasons. First of all, it is a valid problem in itself. Secondly, a study of individual delinquents in a high delinquent area may contribute to the <u>general</u>
understanding of delinquency. Such an area in a sense provides a strategic re-

search site. If there are, in fact, general factors responsible for delinquency then a high delinquent area may prove to be an optimum field of investigation. For here the delinquent-producing factors should exist with greater frequency. Under such conditions of increased concentration it is somewhat easier to detect or uncover these factors. Proportions are not as extremely skewed, thus making statements of inference and association less tenuous. In addition, in multivariate analysis there is less likelihood that the factors would be exhausted by extensive breakdowns. For example, if being a delinquent were strongly associated with female dominant households, one would find the number of such households small in a sample of youths from a general population. Any extensive breakdown of the total sample for any controlling variable (e.g., "broken home") may very well reduce the number of instances of "female dominated households" to such a small size as to make analysis difficult if not impossible One would, under such conditions, need a much larger sample. However, this would not be a severe limitation if one sampled from an area having a fair proportion of female dominated households. Thirdly, the findings of such a study would have important implications for theories of delinquency that include area as an important factor (e.g., sub-cultural theories). (This particular issue will be discussed in greater detail in the final chapter.) Finally, since such areas account for the bulk of official delinquency in large urban areas, certain action implications are suggested. Since a large proportion of funds, time and energy for treatment, prevention and control of delinquency is spent in such areas, knowledge of the delinquency-producing factors could contribute to a more efficient allocation of resources in these areas.

Primarily for pragmatic reasons, it was decided to limit the sample in this study exclusively to Negroes. The study area is predominantly Negro (approximately 72 percent of the area's population in 1960 was Negro) which resulted in a sample heavily weighted with Negroes (87.3 percent of the 1069 youths in the original sample were Negro).[7] This skewed ratio would have made any comparisons between whites and Negroes extremely tenuous, and rather than combine the whites with the Negroes, it was decided to eliminate the whites from the present study in order to achieve a more homogeneous sample. In doing this it was felt that more reliable statements could be made about Negroes rather than a mixed sample. This is especially true concerning factors that have been viewed as having special relevance for Negro behavior (e.g., female dominated households).

What information exists concerning the delinquent and non-delinquent in a high delinquent area?

Perhaps the most widely known attempt to differentiate between the "good" boy and "bad" boy is the research of Reckless and others in a high delinquent area in Columbus, Ohio in 1955.[8]

>...the investigators interviewed all sixth-grade teachers located
>in the highest delinquency areas of predominantly white population.
>The teachers were requested to nominate those white boys in their
>classrooms who would never, in their estimation, experience contact
>with the police or courts. One hundred and ninety-one white boys
>were nominated, comprising approximately one-half of all the white
>boys in the sixth-grade rooms of the elementary schools in the
>highest (predominantly white) areas of delinquency in the city.
>When their names were cleared through the juvenile bureau of the
>police department and the records of the juvenile court, it was

found that in each of 16 instances the boy or a sibling had
been known to the police or court for very minor matters;
these 16 cases were eliminated.[9]

Of the 175 boys, 125 were interviewed. In addition to the "good" boys, 108
"bad" boys were similarly selected by teachers (as "headed for trouble with
the law") about a year later. Of these latter 108 boys, 101 were interviewed,
and 24 of these twelve-year olds had a record for a previous offense. All of
the boys completed a questionnaire consisting of four scales: (1) delinquency
proneness (DE), (2) social responsibility scales of the Gough California Personality inventory (RE), (3) occupational preference, and (4) boy's conception
of self, his family and other interpersonal relationships. On the basis of
their findings, they concluded that isolation from contacts with delinquents
and self images as "good" and "law-abiding" boys insulated the good boy from
becoming delinquent in a high delinquent area.

> ...a good self concept, undoubtedly a product of favorable
> socialization, veers slum boys away from delinquency, while
> a poor self concept, a product of unfavorable socialization,
> gives the slum boy no resistance to deviancy, delinquent com-
> panions, or delinquent subculture. We feel that components
> of the self strength, such as favorable concept of self, act
> as an inner buffer or inner containment against deviancy,
> distraction, lure, and pressures.[10]

These studies have been criticized by Wilkins[11] and Tangri and Schwartz[12] primarily for their use of teachers as the selection device. This means, there
was a lack of independence between the teachers' subjective evaluation of the
student proneness for delinquency and objective knowledge of the boy's record.
It is quite conceivable that the teacher already knows, to a certain extent,
which boys had contact with the police or juvenile court. Consequently, instead of choosing boys entirely on the belief or likelihood of their becoming
delinquents, the teacher has chosen those whom she already knows to be delinquent (or not delinquent, in the case of "good" boys). In addition, the teachers
may have made their selection on the basis of factors which they believed were
associated with delinquency; factors which may consequently have been found by
the researchers to be important for potential delinquency. As Wilkins expresses it:

> The rabbit which was produced from the hat was perhaps placed
> there in the first instance by the unwitting teachers....[13]

In other words, the researchers may have found factors in their analysis which
the teachers thought to be associated with delinquency rather than what was in
actuality associated with delinquency.

It is difficult to understand why Reckless and his associates used teachers
to select the "good" boys and "bad" boys. This procedure seems completely unnecessary and in fact produces a potentially serious flaw in the research design. The more simple, direct and methodologically correct procedure would have
been to use a probability sample of youths who are subsequently separated into
"bad" boys and "good" boys on the basis of the DE scale.

In addition to the methodological flaw, the research primarily utilized

3

social-psychological variables and was concerned only with whites. Thus it is not known if the ecologically important demographic variables would differentiate the delinquent from the non-delinquent or if their findings would hold true for Negro youths.

There have been a few studies employing probability samples in high delinquent areas, namely the investigations of Reiss and Rhodes,[14] Clark and Wenninger,[15] and Hardt and Peterson.[16] All of these studies, with the exception of Reiss and Rhodes, have used in one way or another a sample of Negro boys in high delinquent areas. The one exception dealt only with whites. Clark and Wenninger used self reports as their measure of delinquency, Reiss and Rhodes, juvenile court record, and the work of Hardt employed both self report and police contact.[17] All the researchers investigated only two or three independent variables (namely socio-economic ones). Although their findings will be discussed in greater detail in Chapter Four, the important conclusion should be noted now that they were unable, on the basis of these variables, to differentiate between delinquents and non-delinquents in a high delinquent area.

It seems, therefore, that little is known about the delinquent and non-delinquent in a high delinquent area. We have some limited social psychological evidence from the work of Reckless and others, although their conclusions have to be viewed with caution because of the methodological limitations cited earlier. However, almost no information exists, with the exception of two or three socio-economic factors, concerning the demographic variables that ecological research has found important (e.g., overcrowding, "broken home", home ownership).[18]

In sum, the problem of distinguishing between the delinquent and non-delinquent within a high delinquent, predominantly Negro area has received little systematic attention. The problem seems to be a fairly important one for reasons cited above. This study will investigate this problem by evaluating several "hard" demographic variables which have been, for the most part, suggested by ecological research to have possible relevance for the problem at hand.

I. METHODOLOGY

The principle method employed in this study is secondary analysis of a larger survey research project, known as the North Philadelphia Project. This project was under the sponsorship of the Philadelphia Council for Community Advancement[19] and was primarily concerned with studying social problems (delinquency, health, educational and occupational aspirations, and family relationships) of youth in a "depressed" area of the city. The geographic locus of the study population is an area referred to as North Philadelphia[20] comprising 41 contiguous census tracts (1960 U.S. Census) covering 9.88 square miles (7.6 percent of the total city). It is predominantly Negro, lower income and has more than its share of juvenile delinquents residing in the area.[21]

The sample of youths was drawn from a universe of male youths, 13-15, residing in the area between June 1963 and September 1963.[22] In addition to interviewing the youths, one adult member of the youth's household was also interviewed. In all there were 1098 youths interviewed. After eliminating 136 whites, 21 Negro youths because of no adult interview, and 20 others for various reasons,[23] 921 Negro youths and their corresponding adult interviews was the final sample employed in the present study. With the exception of delinquency status and home ownership, all the data in this study was obtained from the youth and/or adult interviews. The determination of delinquency status was made by a search of official records, and data on home ownership was gathered by the present author three years after the completion of the interviewing.

Two measures of association are employed. For measurement of statistical significance, chi square, and for strength of association, Goodmand and Kruskal's Tau b.[24] The use of chi square is warranted because it is obviously important for making inferential statements; to distinguish between "true" association and sampling variability. However, consideration of significance as the ultimate concern is grossly inadequate, especially for the task at hand. (Since the main task is to distinguish between delinquents and non-delinquents, it is fairly obvious that some attention should be paid to "how well" or efficiently the task is performed.) It is quite possible that "significant" relationships are trivial. An independent variable could explain less than one percent of the variance and still have a probability of occuring by chance of less than one in a hundred. Such a relationship would be far from salient. Despite this seemingly basic consideration of strength of association, surprisingly, a large proportion of research in delinquency, and sociology in general, has been concerned only with tests of significance (especially those that have employed nominal scales). At least this is the subjective impression of the present author. In the desire to evaluate how well the task of discriminating delinquents from non-delinquents in a high delinquent area is carried out, a measure of strength of association was used. Chi square is inappropriate because it is strictly an inferential measure. Measures of association based on chi square (e.g., phi, phi square, Yule's Q, coefficient of contingency) "lack any clear interpretation at all for values other than 0, 1 or the maximum possible given the marginals."[25] The advantage of Goodman and Kruskal's Tau b is that it has a precise operational interpretation or what Costner calls "proportional reduction in error."[26] In formal terms, Costner indicates that a proportional reduction in error measurement is simply:

$$\frac{\text{error B} - \text{error A}}{\text{error B}}$$

Where error A is derived from estimating the value of the dependent variable, knowing the value of the independent variable, and error B is the error from estimating the value of the dependent variable without knowledge of the independent variable. For Goodman and Kruskal's Tau b, error B is simply the number of mistakes one would make by random assignment of events to the categories of the dependent variables. The value of error B is found by using only the column marginals. Error A is the number of mistakes made by "reconstruction, by random assignment, the conditional distributions of the dependent variable for each category of the independent variable."[27] If one thinks of "mistakes" as variability, then another way of interpreting Tau b is the proportion of the total variability (error B) accounted for by the independent variable (error A).[28]

II. DEFINITIONS AND MEASUREMENT OF DELINQUENCY

Definitions of delinquency can involve only categories of "official" delinquency or the broader area of "self-reported" delinquency. The former involves the acquisition of a record by a formal governmental agency stating that the youth has violated at least one delinquency statute. With "self-reported" delinquency respondents are asked to recall selected acts which might have resulted in an official record, if known to the appropriate governmental agency. Two major criticisms of "official" delinquency have been offered: (1) it underestimates the "true" incidence of delinquent acts and juvenile offenders, which is certainly correct; and (2) differential apprehension and delinquency labeling by socio-economic class of the youth operates to bias the incidence of delinquency and offenders in the direction of the lower class, a question which still remains problematic.[29]

The "self-report" approach was developed primarily as a response to the above criticisms of "official" delinquency. Although these instruments ("self-report") have been used extensively, it is still not clear that these newer measures have proven to be more useful in the sociological analysis of delinquency and delinquents. For one, there seems to be little information concerning their validity.[30] In addition, some evidence exists that there is an association between reported delinquency and having an official record,[31] thus the two measures cover, in part, the same phenomenon. On the variable of class Hardt and Peterson report that low income neighborhoods with high official delinquent rates do have a larger proportion of youths reporting "more serious" delinquent acts.[32] There is probably no doubt that official delinquency misses a large segment of juvenile offenses and offenders. However, which measure gives the more accurate estimate of the absolute number of offenses and offenders is not the critical issue for an understanding of delinquency. Instead, the critical question is whether "self-reported" delinquency produces a different set of results with a set of independent variables than does the use of "official" delinquency. If the results are the same, then quite obviously little has been gained by the choice of self-reports over official records. The evidence cited above of an association between the two measures would suggest no differences. Even if there are racial and socio-economic biases in "official" delinquency, they would be minimized in the present study. This is true simply because the sample consists of Negro males residing in a lower class area. Thus the homogeniety of the sample reduces the possible distorting effects of these two variables.

The definitions of delinquency employed in this study are all subsumed under "official" delinquency. However, unlike the usual operational definitions of juvenile delinquency used in most studies, a Juvenile Court record is not the measure used herein, but instead a Juvenile Aid Division[33] (hereafter referred to as J.A.D.) record is the measure of delinquency.

In order to fully appreciate why a J.A.D. record is preferable to a court record, it is necessary to present a brief outline of the judiciary processing of juvenile offenders in Philadelphia[34] (see Figure 1.1). Once a juvenile commits an offense, there are two ways in which the youth comes in contact with the J.A.D.: (1) a direct contact by a J.A.D. member in the course of his duties or (2) referral to the J.A.D. by the uniformed police. (It is accepted standard procedure that every time a juvenile is apprehended by the uniformed police, the J.A.D. is brought into the case.)[35] Some offenders, of course, never become known to the J.A.D. or other agencies and consequently fail to receive a J.A.D. record. The J.A.D. officer has the legal powers either to "remedial" the case (i.e., dismiss the youth with warning that he now has an official record and will be watched in the future) or "arrest" the

FIGURE 1.1   JUDICIAL PROCESSING FOR JUVENILE OFFENDERS
             IN PHILADELPHIA

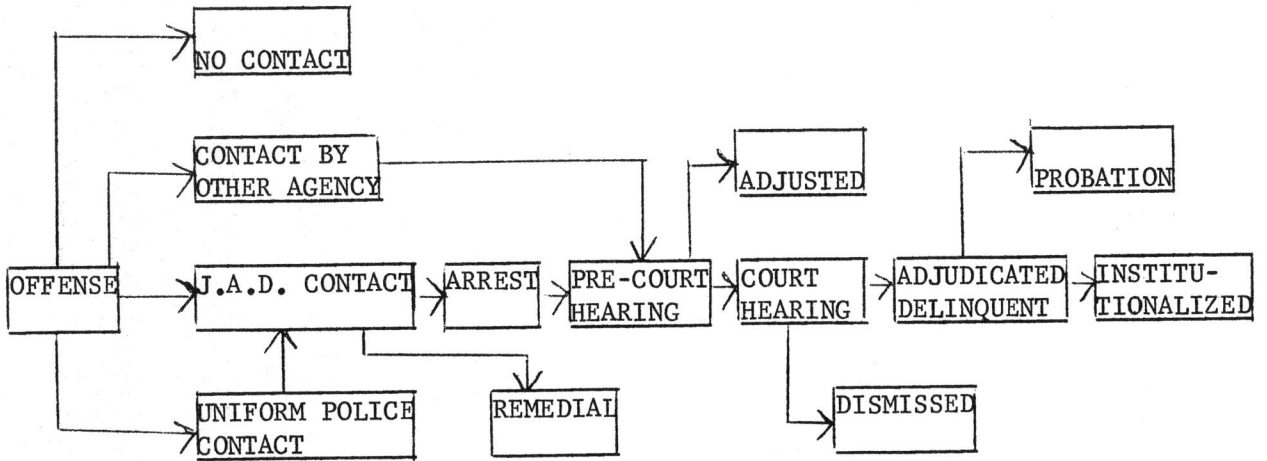

youth (i.e., hold him for further action). In either case he has acquired a J.A.D. record.

What factors are involved in the decision to arrest or remedial? Sellin and Wolfgang, after examining procedures and practices of the Philadelphia J.A.D., state that several factors may be implicated:[36]

(1) the number of previous J.A.D. contacts;

(2) the attitude of the victim (Does he want to prosecute?);

(3) the family situation of the offender;

(4) the attitude of the offender (Is he cooperative, respectful, etc.?);

(5) anticipated disposition of the juvenile court;

(6) the availability of space in the detention centers; and

(7) type of offense (How serious, amount of damage, how much evidence, etc.?)

William Hohenstein,[37] in a multi-variate analysis of decisions made by the Philadelphia J.A.D. to remedial or arrest, found the most important variable to be attitude of the victim. In 78 percent of the cases where the victim made no statement or was in favor of prosecution, an arrest was made, whereas in only 4 percent of the cases where the victim was against prosecution was the juvenile arrested. Previous record, seriousness of the offense, and race of the offender were the only other variables he found to be important. The variable of offender's race accounts for only a very small portion of the total variability of the sample (less than 3 percent). This variable proved important only for those instances where the victim was neutral or for prosecution, the offender was a recidivist, the offense involved was a less serious one, and the offender had no previous arrest. There were only 18 cases having all these characteristics, compared with a total sample size of 501 offenses. Thus the race of the offender became important only after these other variables had operated to explain a major portion of the variability. A study in Santa Monica, California reports similar results to the Hohenstein study.[38] The decision involved here was to "counsel and release" or "petition the juvenile court" similar to the remedial or arrest procedure in Philadelphia. The California study found seriousness of offense, sex, age, previous number of offenses, family situation (intact or broken), probation status, police department (several legal jurisdictions were involved in the study) and year the offense was committed, to have significant zero-order associations with the dependent variable. Race of the offender was not significant. (Unfortunately, the researchers did not include in their study the attitude of the victim or any other characteristics of the victim.) The findings concerning year of offense and police department probably reflect differential police activity. Thus both studies indicate that factors other than characteristics of the offender are involved in whether or not he will appear in court. A juvenile court record is a reflection of arbitrary administrative decisions as well as the characteristics of the offender and the offense.[39]

Once the juvenile is arrested he is given a pre-court hearing, or what is often referred to as an "intake" interview. It is at this point where non-J.A.D. petitions (parents, railway police and school authorities) enter the judiciary process. The primary purposes of this hearing are; (1) to determine if the youth should be detained or released in custody of his parents; (2) gather information and data for the court hearing; (3) and determine if the case merits a court hearing. "In minor matters with parents, victims, and offender present, a case may be 'adjusted', that is, satisfactorily terminated so that it need not further burden the court."[40] How many are so released, or the criteria employed in such a decision, is not known at present.

As can been seen from Figure 1.1 and mentioned above there are some juveniles who are petitioned directly to juvenile court by agencies or persons other than the J.A.D. Consequently there are some youths who have a juvenile court record and are thus considered delinquents, but who do not have a J.A.D. record. How numerous are these cases? As can be seen from Table 1.1 (statistics given by Philadelphia County Court) the vast bulk of petitions are from the J.A.D. (88.0 percent).

TABLE 1.1. SOURCE OF REFERRALS TO JUVENILE COURT, PHILADELPHIA, 1965

	N	%
Phila. J.A.D.	8213	88.0
Other judiciary agency (probation officer, Youth Study Center, and another court)	254	2.7
Railroad Police	329	3.5
Parent or relative	222	2.4
Individual	138	1.5
School Authorities	161	1.7
Social agency or Institution	19	0.2
Total	9336	100.0

Source: Fifty Second Annual Report of the County Court of Philadelphia, 1965, p. 64.

In the case of two other referring agencies, railroad police and other judiciary agencies, it is likely that these youths would acquire a J.A.D. record. Only with referrals by parents or relatives, individuals, school authorities and social agencies or institutions (5.8 percent of all cases) is it probable that these cases are not noted in the J.A.D. file.[41] (Sellin and Wolfgang report that these referrals are more likely to involve juvenile status offenses such as curfew, truancy, and incorrigibility.)[42]

Sellin[43] has argued that the further the distance from the actual commission of the offense in the judiciary process, the smaller the number of cases[44] and the less valid the measurement of crime. In terms of cases lost, this is certainly true. In the present sample 53.3 percent of the delinquents (having a J.A.D. record) do not have a court record.[45] But the numbers of cases lost is not the critical issue. If the losses were random then the analysis of delinquency with a set of independent variables would not be affected. But is random loss a reasonable assumption? The evidence cited previously on the remedial-arrest decision indicates that the assumption is in fact an unreasonable one. In comparison with criminal procedure the juvenile procedure seems to be effected more by "intervening" factors which are administrative in nature and often unrelated to the delinquency of the offender. For delinquency, persons are legally empowered to dismiss or hold for hearing somewhat independent of the actual guilt of committing the delinquent act. In criminal procedure, where there is sufficient evidence of guilt, no one can legally dismiss a defendent until a final trial has been carried out. By utilizing a J.A.D. record the effect of these and other administrating decisions have been minimized.

One major definition employed throughout this study is the existence of any J.A.D. record (whether or not the boy was either arrested, adjudicated delinquent or institutionalized) and will be referred to as Definition I.

It can be argued that all delinquents should not be considered to be members of a homogeneous group. A youth who murders or rapes is probably very different from one whose most serious official misdeed is the violation of a curfew. Juveniles committing the more serious offenses may be said to be "true" delinquents (or juvenile criminals), whereas those committing the less serious ones are simply boys expending youthful energy who have the misfortune of being caught.[46] In order to consider this, a meaningful operational definition of delinquency should be based upon the most serious offense a youth has committed (as this is known to the J.A.D.). Before this can be done, there must be some agreement as to the relative seriousness of delinquent actions.

Sellin and Wolfgang[47] conclude that a scheme for ordering seriousness of offenses can be constructed. In decreasing seriousness they are acts which: (1) involve bodily injury and harm; (2) property loss or damage; (3) do not involve bodily harm or property loss or damage, not violate adult criminal laws; (4) violate juvenile laws (truancy, curfew, incorrigibility, etc.). Utilizing the Sellin and Wolfgang rationale, the following "ordering" procedure was employed to define seriousness in this study:

1. The most serious offenses are those which involve physical harm to the victim, property loss or damage (A);
2. Second in seriousness are those acts which did not involve physical harm or property loss or damage but would be considered a crime if committed by an adult (B);
3. Finally, there are those offenses which do not involve physical harm, property loss or damage, and would not be considered a crime if committed by an adult (these are acts prohibited only so long as the offender is under the age of 18). (C)

These three classes will be referred to as A,B and C delinquencies, respectively and each of the juvenile offenders in our sample was classified according to the most serious offense listed on his J.A.D. record. The specific offense falling within each category are: class A, rape, robbery, assault and battery (aggravated and non-aggravated), burglary, larceny (all dollar values) and malicious mischief; class B, weapons, sex offenses (non-commercial) and disorderly conduct and street corner lounging; and class C, runaway, truancy and curfew.[48] The distribution of offenders by most serious offense for this study is listed in Table 1.2.

TABLE 1.2.   DISTRIBUTION OF OFFENDERS BY
MOST SERIOUS OFFENSE.

TYPE OF OFFENSE	N	%
Class A - Person-Property	212	59.4
Class B - Non (Person-Property, Juvenile status)	73	20.4
Class C - Juvenile Status	72	20.2
Total	357	100.0

The largest number of offenders consisted of those who had committed a person-property offense as their most serious offense. If the assumption is made that crimes against the person are more serious than crimes against property, then the bulk of Class A offenders (72.6 percent) were property offenders.

The labeling of offenses committed by juveniles, is done by the police and/or J.A.D. personnel. To what extent are these sometimes arbitrary lables valid (i.e., do they reflect the kinds of behavior that have been used to define seriousness in Classes A, B and C?). Sellin and Wolfgang[49] compared the official labels made by the police with the acts as classified according to their criteria (physical harm, property loss, etc.) There was agreement in over 95% of the cases (Table 1.3). (Only those offenses which are found in the sample of the present study are listed.) It would seem therefore, that the use of the official J.A.D. classifications does allow for a fairly accurate classification according to the seriousness schema discussed above. However, in order to apply the same conclusion to the data for the present sample the distribution of offenders in Table 1.3 must be similar to that of the delinquent population in the present study. The three sub-classes in Table 1.3 have different "error rates", which means that the total "error rate" is the weighted sum of the three sub-totals. (The weights being the proportion of delinquents in each sub-class) The Sellin and Wolfgang analysis can only support the present data if the "weights" are same, in other words, the distribution of offenders for each sub-class in Table 1.3 is similar to those for this study. Fortunately, the two distributions are similar. Table 1.3 shows 53.3 percent of all delinquents are in Class A, 22.4 percent in Class B and 24.2 percent in Class C. The distribution in this study is 59.4 percent, 20.4 percent and 20.2 percent, respectively (Table 1.2).

In addition to Definition I (presence of any J.A.D. record), two additional definitions, based upon most serious offense in the J.A.D. record are used. They are Definition II, having committed an offense against the person or property as the most serious misdeed, and Definition III, any offense with exception of a juvenile status offense. (This latter definition, therefore, includes those offenses which would be legally defined as crimes if committed by an adult.)

TABLE 1.3. COMPARISON OF CLASSIFICATIONS, POLICE VS. RESEARCH CATEGORY,* FOR OFFENDERS, PHILADELPHIA, 1960.

OFFENSE	TOTAL	NOT CONFORMING TO RESEARCH CATEGORY	
		N	%
Rape	11	4	36.4
Robbery	62	7	11.3
Assault and battery	207	7	3.4
Burglary	154	12	7.8
Larceny	353	9	2.5
Malicious Mischief	120	30	25.0
Class A - Subtotal	(907)	(69)	(7.6)
Weapons	44	0	0.0
Sex offenses (non-commercial)	53	5	9.4
Disorderly Conduct	284	5	1.8
Class B - Subtotal	(381)	(10)	(2.6)
Runaway	245	0	0.0
Truancy	168	0	0.0
Curfew	Not included in Sellin-Wolfgang Study		
Class C - Subtotal	(413)	(0)	(0.0)
Total	1701	79	4.6

*Research categories are: Class A - property loss, damage or physical harm; Class B - no property loss or damage and no physical harm; Class C - juvenile status offenses and no property loss or damage and no physical harm. A non-conforming case would be one which violated the conditions of the class it was a part of. (E.g., a case of disorderly conduct which involved physical harm or property loss or damage would be a non-conforming case.)

Source: Thoreston Sellin and Marvin E. Wolfgang, The Measurement of Delinquency, New York: John Wiley and Sons, 1964, pp. 161-163.

III. ORGANIZATION OF STUDY

Before beginning the main task of this study it is necessary to indicate, with some degree of precision, that the study area has those characteristics which the ecological research has found to be correlated with high delinquent rates. This is the purpose of Chapter Two, <u>Demographic Description of the Study Area</u>. The set of demographic variables being investigated in this study have been divided into two general categories; family structure and socio-economic variables. Family structure is covered in Chapter Three and includes the variables of presence of parents, presence of adult males, sex of household head, sex of main wage earner, sex of adult who influences the youth most, sex of main decision maker, (the last four variables are used as indicators of matri-archy), household size and ordinal position. The socio-economic variables are analyzed in Chapter Four and includes occupation and education of main wage earner, home ownership and room density. In addition to the separate analysis of these two general areas there will be some attempt to combine the two, in a limited way, in Chapter Four.

The rationale in Chapters Three and Four will be first to indicate in what manner the variable in question may be involved in delinquent etiology. Sec-ondly empirical findings from previous studies will be summarized. Since, as mentioned previously, there has been little research directed to studying de-linquency in a delinquent area, much of the review of previous findings invol-ves studies of a more general population. Finally each of the variables will be tested for how well they can distinguish the delinquent from the non-delin-quent. However this is not the end result of the analysis. In the case of some of the variables a partial association analysis will be conducted. By doing this the problem can be investigated in a more intensive manner.

The last chapter will suggest several alternative explanations for the findings of this study. These interpretations will not only be concerned with explaining delinquency in a high delinquent area, but in a limited manner they will be concerned with implications for the general study of delinquency.

Footnotes:

1. Clifford Shaw, _et al._, _Delinquency Areas_, Chicago: University of Chicago Press, 1929. See also Clifford Shaw and Henry D. McKay, _Juvenile Delinquency and Urban Areas_, Chicago: University of Chicago Press, 1942.

2. A listing of these studies is given in Chapter 2, p. 51, note 16.

3. W. S. Robinson, "Ecological Correlations and the Behavior of Individuals", _American Sociological Review_, 15 (June, 1950), pp. 351-357.

4. Herbert Menzal, "Comment on Robinson's 'Ecological Correlations and the Behavior of Individuals'," _American Sociological Review_, 15 (October, 1950), p. 674.

5. Leo A. Goodman, "Some Alternatives to Ecological Correlation", _The American Journal of Sociology_, 64 (May, 1959), pp. 610-625.

6. Two variables are included in this study which have, as best as can be determined, never been used directly in ecological studies of delinquency. They are female-dominated households and ordinal position of the youth. The apparent reason for this is the unavailability, on a tract basis, of census data for these two variables. The reason for including female-dominated households is the fairly prevalent notion that such a factor is a critical one in explaining the high delinquent rates in certain areas. Ordinal position was included because of its possible effect on other variables in this study (e.g., "broken home" and female dominated households).

7. There may be several factors to account for the difference between the population and the sample value for the proportion of Negroes: (1) a time difference, the population value is for 1960, the same was drawn in 1963; (2) the sample consists of young Negro males (13-15 years) and since the Negro population in the area is considerably younger than the white population (in 1960 the median age for Negro males was 24 and 42 for white males) there would be a large proportion of Negroes in the 13-15 year old population; and finally of course (3) sample variability.

8. Walter C. Reckless, Simon Dinitz and Ellen Murray, "Self Concept as an Insulator against Delinquency", _American Sociological Review_, 21 (December, 1956), pp. 744-746; Reckless, Dinitz and Murray, "The 'Good' Boy in a High Delinquency Area", _Journal of Criminal Law, Criminology and Police Science_, 48 (August, 1957), pp. 18-26; Reckless, Dinitz and Barbara Kay, "The Self-Component in Potential Delinquency and Potential Non-Delinquency", _American Sociological Review_, 22 (October, 1957), pp. 566-570; Dinitz, Kay and Reckless, "Group Gradients in Delinquency Potential and Achievement Scores of Sixth Graders", _American Journal of Orthopsychiatry_, 28 (July, 1958), pp. 588-605; Dinitz, Reckless and Kay, "A Self-Gradient amoung Potential Delinquents", _Journal of Criminal Law, Criminology and Police Science_, 49 (May, 1958), pp. 230-233; John E. Simpson, Dinitz, Kay and Reckless, "Delinquency Potential of Pre-Adolescents in High Delinquency Areas", _British Journal of Delinquency_, 10 (January, 1963), pp. 211-215; Frank Scarpitti, Murray, Dinitz and Reckless, "The 'Good' Boy in a High Delinquency Area: Four Years Later", _American Sociological Review_, 25 (August,

1960), pp. 555-558; Dinitz, Scarpitti and Reckless, "Delinquency Vulner-
ability: A Group and Longitudinal Analysis", American Sociological Review,
27 (August, 1962), pp. 515-517.

　　　For general review and criticism of these studies, see Sandra S.
Tangri and Michael Schwartz, "Delinquency Research and the Self-Concept
Variable", The Journal of Criminal Law, Criminology and Police Science,
58 (October, 1967), pp. 182-190.

9.　Scarpitti, et al. (1960), op. cit., p. 555.

10.　Dinitz, et al. (1962), op. cit., p. 517.

11.　Leslie T. Wilkins, "Juvenile Delinquency: A Critical Review of Research
and Theory", Educational Research, 5 (February, 1963), pp. 104-119.

12.　Tangri and Schwartz, op. cit.

13.　Wilkins, op. cit., p. 116.

14.　Albert J. Reiss and Albert Lewis Rhodes, "Delinquency and Social Class
Structure", American Sociological Review, 26 (October, 1961), pp. 720-732.

15.　John P. Clark and Eugene P. Wenninger, "Socio-Economic Class and Area as
Correlates of Illegal Behavior among Juveniles", American Sociological
Review, 27 (December, 1962), pp. 826-834.

16.　Robert H. Hardt and Sandra J. Peterson, "Neighborhood Status and Delinquency Activity as Indexed by Police Records and a Self-Report Survey",
unpublished paper presented at the Eastern Sociological Society Meetings,
Boston, 1964; Robert H. Hardt, "Delinquency and Social Class: Studies of
Juvenile Deviations or Police Disposition?" unpublished paper presented
at the Eastern Sociological Society meetings, New York, 1965.

17.　The definitions and measures of delinquency will be discussed in detail
later in this chapter.

18.　Some of the so-called "hard" variables employed in this study can be interpreted in a social-psychological framework and, in fact, is done so at
various points in this study.

　　　No criticism that social psychological variables are not important
is intended here. The only concern is to determine if the "hard" variables
will be important for the problem at hand with no implicit assumption that
other variables could not be important as well.

19.　A non-profit action research agency, receiving its major support from the
Ford Foundation and the President's Committee on Juvenile Delinquency.

20.　The exact geographic boundaries are given in the Appendix, p. 123.

21.　These characteristics, along with others, will be documented with more
precision in the following chapter.

22.　The sampling procedure is described in the Appendix, p. 123.

23. See Appendix, p. 123.

24. Leo A. Goodman and William H. Kruskal, "Measures of Association for Cross Classifications", <u>Journal of the American Statistical Association</u>, 49 (December, 1954), pp. 732-764.

25. Herbert L. Costner, "Criteria for Measures of Association", <u>American Sociological Review</u>, 30 (June, 1965), p. 351. The 2 x 2 case provides for an exception, as will be seen below.

26. <u>Ibid</u>., pp. 341-353.

27. <u>Ibid</u>., p. 351.

28. In a 2 x 2 table Tau b is the same as phi square. Thus phi square is interpretable in proportionate reduction of error terms; however, this is only possible because it is equivalent to Tau b (Costner, op. cit., p. 352). Since chi square, in a 2 x 2, is related to phi square $X^2 = \emptyset^2 N$ it is possible, in a sense, to view chi square in the same terms as Tau b. However, this is always conditioned by total sample size (N). It is also clearly seen why, in a 2 x 2 table, the size of chi square is affected directly by the sample size. Thus, the larger the sample, the more sensitive chi square is in detecting small degrees of association in the total population.

29. The following "self-report" studies have found to relationship between delinquency and social-class: Austin L. Porterfield, <u>Youth in Trouble</u>, Fort Worth, Texas: Leo Potishman Foundation, (1946); F. Ivan Nye, James P. Short, Jr., and Virgil J. Olson, "Socio-Economic Status and Delinquent Behavior", <u>American Journal of Sociology</u>, 63 (January, 1958), pp. 381-389; Robert A. Dentler and Lawrence J. Monroe, "Social Correlates of Early Adolescent Theft", <u>American Sociological Review</u>, 26 (October, 1961), pp. 733-743; John P. Clark and Eugene P. Wenninger, <u>op</u>. <u>cit</u>.; Ronald L. Akers, "Socio-Economic Status and Delinquent Behavior: A Retest", <u>Journal of Research on Crime and Delinquency</u>, 1 (January, 1964), pp. 38-46.
     The following "self-report" studies have found a negative relationship between social class and delinquency: Albert J. Reiss, Jr. and Albert L. Rhodes, <u>op</u>. <u>cit</u>.; Maynard L. Erickson and LaMar T. Empey, "Class Position, Peers, and Delinquency", <u>Sociology and Social Research</u>, 49 (April, 1965), pp. 269-282; Martin Gold, "Undetected Delinquent Behavior", <u>Journal of Research in Crime and Delinquency</u>, 3 (January, 1966), pp. 27-46. Harwin L. Ross, "Socio-Economic Status and Reported Delinquent Behavior", <u>Social Problems</u>, 13 (Winter, 1966), pp. 314-324, reports a positive relationship, however this study has been criticized by Martin Gold, "On Social Status and Delinquency", <u>Social Problems</u>, 15 (Summer, 1967), pp. 114-116, as loads its delinquency scale with "non-chargeable trivia", acts which upper class boys are more likely to commit.

30. Robert H. Hardt and George E. Bodine, Development of <u>Self-Reporting Instruments in Delinquency Research</u>, Syracuse, New York: Youth Development Center, Syracuse University, 1965.

31. Hardt and Bodine, <u>op</u>. <u>cit</u>., p. 13 and Robert E. Hardt, (1965), <u>op</u>. <u>cit</u>

32. Hardt and Peterson, op. cit.

33. An official unit of the Philadelphia Police Department. The unit is comprised of several subunits, of which the major ones are: (1) line squad, whose primary responsibility is to investigate all cases of juveniles referred to them by uniformed police; (2) gang control squad, they are responsible for surveillance and control of "troublesome" juvenile groups in the city; and (3) morals squad who investigate sex offenses committed by juveniles.

34. This discussion is based on (1) Thorsten Sellin and Marvin E. Wolfgang, The Measurement of Delinquency, New York: John Wiley and Sons, 1964, Chapter 7, and (2) Fifty Second Annual Report of the County Court of Philadelphia, 1965.

35. Sellin and Wolfgang report that some juvenile cases are disposed of by the uniformed police without notification of the J.A.D.; however, they feel that the number of such cases is extremely small. Sellin and Wolfgang, op. cit., p.107.

36. Ibid., pp. 95-100.

37. In Thorsten Sellin and Marvin E. Wolfgang, (Editors), Studies in Delinquency, New York: John Wiley and Sons, in press. The independent variables employed were: age of offender, race of offender, sex of offender, number of previous arrests, seriousness of the offense, race of victim, and the attitude of victim towards prosecution.

38. A. W. McEachern and Riva Bauzer, "Factors Related to Disposition in Juvenile Police Contacts", in Malcolm W. Klein (Editor), Juvenile Gangs in Context, Englewood Cliffs, New Jersey: Prentice-Hall, Inc., 1967, pp. 148-160.

39. From this discussion it is obvious that the decision to remedial does not necessarily imply a serious offense. Sellin and Wolfgang (op. cit., (1964), p. 195 and p. 218) report predictability of disposition from seriousness of offense to be low. This same result is found with the present sample.

40. Ibid., p. 91.

41. This does not necessarily mean that youths who are referred by these sources do not possess J.A.D. records. The referrals listed in Table 1.1 are not only for first offenders. This means that a youth with a previous J.A.D. record may have been petitioned to the court by the non-J.A.D. referral for one offense in 1965. This would reduce, even further, the number of youths who would not have a J.A.D. record. How many such cases are in Table 1.1 cannot be determined, but it seems likely that the number of youths petitioned to court who do not have a J.A.D. record is even smaller than the data in Table 1.1 would indicate.

42. Sellin and Wolfgang, (1964), op. cit., p. 57.

43. Thorsten Sellin, "The Significance of Records of Crime", <u>The Law Quarterly Review</u>, 67 (October, 1951), pp. 489-504.

44. For adult criminal procedure Van Vechten has demonstrated a large reduction of cases as one proceeds further into the judicial process. See Courtland C. Van Vechten, "Criminal Case Mortality", <u>American Sociological Review</u>, 7 (December, 1942), pp. 833-839.

45. This figure is probably not completely correct, because only J.A.D. records were consulted. If the previous discussion is correct, we would expect a slightly lower percentage because of non-J.A.D. court referrals.

46. As Cyril Burt expresses it: "There is, however, no sharp line of cleavage by which the delinquent may be marked off from the non-delinquent. Between them no deep gulf exists to separate the sinner from the saint, the white sheet from the black. It is all a problem of degree, of a brighter or a darker grey....they run in an uninterrupted series, from the most heartless and persistent crimes that could possibly be pictured, up to the more occasional naughtiness to which the most virtuous will at times give way." (Cyril Burt, <u>The Young Delinquent</u>, Third edition, London: University of London Press, 1938, pp. 14-15)

47. Sellin and Wolfgang (1964), <u>op</u>. <u>cit</u>., Chapter 10. The rationale presumably underlying this scheme is that in our society seriousness is measured in terms of physical injury, rather than property damage. (Death > bodily injury > property loss > acts not involving harm to the body or property, i.e., victimless crimes.) The seriousness scale was validated by respondents rating various crimes. (See Chapters 15-18.)

48. Many classification schemes have been suggested over time. One interesting one, by Burt, consist of: (1) sex; (2) anger (murder wounding, bad temper, etc.); (3) acquisitiveness (stealing, begging, etc.); (4) wandering (truancy, runaway, etc.); (5) grief (attempted suicide and threatened suicide); and (6) secretiveness (lying). Burt, <u>op</u>. <u>cit</u>., pp. 15-16.

49. Sellin and Wolfgang (1964), <u>op</u>. <u>cit</u>., pp. 156-164. The data is based on a 10 percent sample of all juvenile offenses in 1960 known to the Philadelphia J.A.D.

CHAPTER TWO

Demographic Description of Study Area[1]

The aim of this chapter is two-fold: (1) precise documentation, that the
area is a high delinquent and predominantly Negro area; (2) to indicate that
the area possesses those qualities which the ecological research has shown to
be associated with high delinquent rates. Both of these aims necessitate a
comparison of the area with the total city or the remainder of the city for
each variable in question. In addition, since the present study is concerned
with Negroes, comparisons of Negroes with whites should be useful as well (although it was impossible to make such comparisons for all of the factors discussed).

The study area[2] is fairly typical of many other low income, largely Negro
areas in large cities. It contains a higher incidence of practically all of
the "classic" social problems: Crime and delinquency, poverty, unemployment,
poor housing, overcrowding, broken families, low education, illegitimacy, and
unskilled workers among others. While there may be debate on whether such an
area can be characterized as "organized or disorganized", there is consensus
that "something" is operating in these kinds of areas which produce a high delinquency rate.

I. POPULATION

As of 1960 there were approximately 330,000 persons (see Table 2.1) in the
study area, which represented 16 percent of the city's population. The area
has lost 13.0 percent of its population (see Table 2.2) from 1950 to 1960, compared with a 1.3 percent loss in the remainder of the city, primarily, a result
of extensive urban renewal in the area. The area is predominantly Negro, with
44.0 percent of the Philadelphia non-whites and 6.4 percent of the city's whites
residing in the area. The area has been losing whites and adding non-whites at
a faster rate than the remainder of the city (Table 2.2). This differential
change of the white-non-white distribution is reflected in the indices of residential segregation.[3] For 1960 the index in the area was 61.4, an increase of
1.7 since 1950 and 5.6 since 1940. The city experienced an increase of 5.2
from 1950 to 1960 (from 73.3 to 78.5).[4] This general trend toward increasing
segregation has been documented for other large cities.[5] Although the segregation index in the area has not changed drastically within the 20-year period,
the majority population has changed from white to Negro. Thus the area has gone
from a highly segregated white area with Negro enclaves to a highly segregated
Negro area with white enclaves. It is also interesting to note that the segregation index for the area is lower than the city which implies that in this
Negro ghetto, the dispersion of whites is more uniform than the dispersion of
Negroes within the white population for the total city.

The area is also quite densely populated, being twice as dense as the total
city (33,243 persons/square mile vs. 15,424 persons/square mile).[6]

II. SOCIO-ECONOMIC CHARACTERISTICS

Median family income in the area is, as expected, below that of the total city ($3,382 vs. $4,789), with the non-whites being lower than whites in both the city and the area. However, Negro-white income differential is smaller in the area. The ratio of median total income to median non-white income being 1.08 for the area and 1.42 for the total city. In addition, the income spread is tighter in the area; the inter-quartile range is $3,709 in the area and $4,360 for the total city.

Unemployment, i.e., percent of labor force unemployed, in the area was about twice as high as the total city. For males the percentages are 11.4 percent and 6.4 percent respectively, with the corresponding percentages for females being 10.6 and 6.2.[7]

The changes in the occupational structure (Table 2.3)[8] reflect some of the crucial aspects of the 1950 to 1960 population changes in the area and the city For one, the city experienced a decline in high prestige jobs[9] primarily as the result of a relative loss of managers and craftsmen-foremen. The increase in low prestige jobs is due almost entirely to an increase of unreported jobs (it is assumed that unreported occupations are primarily made up of unskilled labor).[10] The total study area exhibits the same trends, but to a greater degree. All high prestige positions decreased in relative proportion, and almost all low prestige positions increased.

The area non-white's pattern differed somewhat from the trends in the city and the total study area. Increases from 1950 to 1960 were noted in the high prestige jobs mainly in the clerical positions and to a lesser extent craftsmen-foremen. However, the professional and managerial categories decreased. Within the low prestige category of non-whites, laborers and service workers lost sufficiently enough to override the gain of the operatives and unreported occupations. In general, therefore, the occupational structure of the non-whites in the area was slightly upgraded, primarily through increases in the middle range (clerical, sales, craftsmen and foremen) and decreases in the unskilled (laborer and service).[11] This trend for non-whites is counter to the trend for the whites in the area and the total population in the city.

The whites in the study area are the ones who have experienced the most drastic change. Whereas in 1950 the area's white distribution was very similar to the total city, it departed more radically from the city average in 1960. Among area whites, all high prestige jobs, with the exception of professional, exhibited reductions, and all low prestige ones, except operatives, gained.

A comparison of the relative changes for whites and non-whites in the area can be seen from Table 2.4

TABLE 2.1.   DISTRIBUTION OF WHITES AND NON-WHITES WITHIN STUDY
             AREA AND REMAINDER OF CITY: 1940, 1950 AND 1960.

	STUDY AREA		REMAINDER OF CITY	
YEAR	N	% of Area[1]	N	% of Remainder[2]
		WHITES		
1940	231,869	70.4	1,446,708	70.3
1950	223,175	59.1	1,469,462	86.7
1960	93,288	28.4	1,372,191	82.1
		NON-WHITES		
1940	97,634	29.6	155,123	9.7
1950	154,514	40.9	224,454	13.3
1960	235,156	71.6	299,877	17.9
		TOTAL		
1940	329,503	100.0	1,601,831	100.0
1950	377,689	100.0	1,693,916	100.0
1960	328,444	100.0	1,672,068	100.0

[1]The figures cited here are for the percentage of the total population
in the study area.

[2]The figures cited here are for the percentage of the total population
in the remainder of the city.

NOTE: The frequencies for 1950 are different than those given in the
        Fact Book (see note 1). The discrepancies apparently are due to
        the failure of the Fact Book to correctly incorporate the changes
        of tract boundaries within the study area from 1950 to 1960.
        The figures for 1940 were compiled by the author for this study.

TABLE 2.2   PERCENT CHANGE OF WHITES AND NON-WHITES WITHIN STUDY
AREA AND REMAINDER OF CITY; 1940-1950, 1950-1960
AND 1940-1960.

	1940-1950	1950-1960	1940-1960
STUDY AREA			
White	- 3.7	-58.2	-59.8
Non-White	+58.2	+52.9	+140.8
Total Population	+14.6	-13.0	- 3.2
REMAINDER OF CITY			
White	+ 1.6	- 6.6	- 5.2
Non-White	+44.7	+25.2	+93.3
Total Population	+ 5.7	- 1.3	+ 4.4

TABLE 2.3. OCCUPATIONAL DISTRIBUTION (PERCENT OF EMPLOYED MALES) OF MALES FOR NON-WHITE AND WHITE STUDY AREA AND TOTAL PHILADELPHIA, 1950 AND 1960.

	STUDY AREA				PHILADELPHIA	
OCCUPATION	NON-WHITE		WHITE		TOTAL	
	1950	1960	1950	1960	1950	1960
HIGH PRESTIGE						
Professional	2.0	1.9	6.2	7.5	7.7	9.0
Managerial	2.9	1.8	9.4	6.5	10.6	8.2
Clerical	5.8	7.7	10.7	9.8	9.6	10.7
Sales	2.1	2.2	7.8	6.2	7.6	7.2
Craftsmen-Foremen	11.5	12.0	24.6	18.6	21.9	19.3
Sub-Total	(24.3)	(25.6)	(58.7)	(48.6)	(57.9)	(54.4)
LOW PRESTIGE						
Operatives	26.9	30.3	25.9	24.9	23.6	23.0
Private Household	0.8	0.5	0.1	*	0.2	0.2
Service Workers	15.6	13.9	8.8	10.4	8.9	9.0
Laborer	30.6	18.4	5.1	6.6	8.3	7.0
Unreported	1.8	11.2	1.4	9.4	1.1	6.4
Sub-Total	(75.7)	(74.4)	(41.3)	(51.3)	(42.2)	(45.6)
TOTAL	100.0	100.0	100.0	99.9	100.1	100.0
Total Number	33,552	45,938	57,220	23,482	552,711	498,017

*Less than 0.1

TABLE 2.4. THE RELATIVE OCCUPATIONAL STRUCTURE OF WHITES AND
NON-WHITES IN THE STUDY AREA, 1950 AND 1960

OCCUPATION	RATIO OF PROPORTION OF EMPLOYED WHITE MALES TO PROPORTION OF EMPLOYED NON-WHITE MALES	
	1950	1960
HIGH PRESTIGE	(2.42)	(1.90)
Professional	2.95	3.95
Managerial	3.13	3.61
Clerical	1.84	1.27
Sales	3.71	2.82
Craftsmen-Foremen	2.14	1.55
LOW PRESTIGE	(0.54)	(0.70)
Operatives	0.96	0.82
Private Household	0.12	0.06
Service Workers	0.56	0.75
Laborer	0.17	0.36
Unreported	0.78	0.84

The general picture is that the two occupational structures are more similar
in 1960 than in 1950. Since the non-white distributions show more stability
over time than the white distribution, the greater similarity in 1960 can be
attributed mainly to a down-grading of the white occupational structure.

A closer look at some of the specific occupational groups indicates some
interesting trends. For one, the white professionals in the area increased
their relative share of the occupational distribution, whereas the managerial
and skilled workers lost. (There was an actual loss in the number of white
professionals, 3,532 to 1,759, but their loss was at a slower rate than the
total loss for the employed white males in the labor force.) The city exhibited a similar trend. Consequently, those whites that are migrating out
of the city are more likely to be managers and officials or skilled workers.
The professionals are either migrating out at a slower rate or are showing a
greater tendency to move back into the city.[12]

The educational level in the area (Table 2.5) is below that of the city.
The median "school years completed" for the area was 8.8 compared to 9.6 for
the remainder of the city. The area had a lower proportion of college graduates
(2.4 percent vs. 5.6 percent), smaller proportion of those completing at least
high school (20.8 percent vs. 30.0 percent), and a somewhat smaller proportion

of at least grammar school completion (48.1 percent vs. 73.1 percent).

TABLE 2.5. SCHOOL YEARS COMPLETED FOR PERSONS 25 YEARS OLD AND OVER, STUDY AREA, REMAINDER OF CITY, 1960.

	STUDY AREA		REMAINDER OF CITY	
YEARS OF SCHOOLING	N	%	N	%
None	6,395	3.6	34,473	3.3
Elementary: 1 - 4	19,820	11.1	53,904	5.2
5 - 7	34,439	20.9	164,726	16.0
8	32,307	18.0	202,518	19.6
High School: 1 - 3	45,691	25.5	242,448	23.5
4	27,465	15.3	220,645	21.4
College: 1 - 3	5,558	3.1	56,021	5.4
4+	4,379	2.4	57,708	5.6
TOTAL	179,054	99.9	1,032,443	100.0
Median Years Completed	8.8		9.6	

The only educational level approaching equity was for no formal education.

III. FAMILY

The proporation of single persons (14 years and above) in the study area is about the same as that in the rest of the city (Table 2.6).

TABLE 2.6.   MARITAL STATUS OF PERSONS OVER 14 IN STUDY AREA
             AND REMAINDER OF CITY, 1960.

		STUDY AREA		REMAINDER OF CITY	
MARITAL STATUS		N	%	N	%
		ALL PERSONS			
Single		60,615	24.4	322,516	24.6
Married		136,578	55.0	795,881	61.0
Separated		21,645	8.7	39,439	3.0
Widowed		24,363	9.8	126,535	9.6
Divorced		5,264	2.1	25,567	1.9
	TOTAL	248,465	100.0	1,309,938	100.1
		EVER MARRIED			
Married		136,578	72.7	795,881	80.6
Separated		21,645	11.5	39,439	4.0
Divorce		24,363	13.0	126,535	12.8
Widowed		5,264	2.8	25,567	2.6
	TOTAL	187,850	100.0	987,422	100.0

However, the proportion of married in the area is somewhat lower primarily because of a higher separation rate within the area. The marital dissolution rate (divorced and separated) is higher in the area; of the ever-married, the proportion separated or divorced was 24.5 percent for the area and 16.8 percent for the remainder of the city. (The difference is due almost entirely to separations.) It must be remembered that the marital status was that at the time of the census and did not indicate the number of ever-divorced (or for that matter, ever-separated and ever-widowed, also). Thus, there are certainly persons who were at one time divorced but who at the time of the survey could be in any one of the other ever-married categories (married, separated and widowed). A divorce rate on the basis of the ever-divorced might well show differences between the area and the city.

The differential break-up rate, of course, influences the "broken home" rates. The proportion of persons under 18 <u>not</u> living with <u>both</u> parents in the area was 36.9 percent, a figure more than twice as high for the remainder of the city (15.9%). The "broken home" rate is also a consequence of illegitimacy and the illegitimacy rates in the area are about 2.8 times greater than the rest of the city (20.7 percent of all births vs. 7.5 percent). Most of the "broken homes" involve the absence of the father, which would mean a larger proportion of female-head households within the study area. Unfortunately, the census figures for this are not readily available by census tracts; therefore, comparisons cannot be made. However, there is a fair amount of confidence that such a figure would be somewhat higher in the study area.[13]

IV. HOUSING

Philadelphia is unusual among large cities in that it has a somewhat high rate of owner-occupancy (61.9 percent in 1960).

TABLE 2.7. DISTRIBUTION OF OCCUPIED HOUSING UNITS BY TENURE, BY RACE, FOR STUDY AREA AND REMAINDER OF CITY, 1960.

HOUSING TENURE	WHITE		NON-WHITE		TOTAL	
	N	%	N	%	N	%
STUDY AREA						
Owner-Occupied	16,013	48.9	22,674	34.5	38,687	39.3
Renter-Occupied	16,717	51.1	43,058	65.5	59,775	60.7
Total Occupied Units	32,730	100.0	65,732	100.0	98,462	100.0
REMAINDER OF CITY						
Owner-Occupied	301,221	69.4	41,354	49.6	342,525	66.2
Renter-Occupied	132,716	30.6	42,014	50.4	174,730	33.8
Total Occupied Units	433,937	100.0	83,368	100.0	517,255	100.0

Although the ownership rate is smaller in the study area (see Table 2.7), it still is high in comparison to other cities, such as New York, San Francisco, Chicago and Boston, but is somewhat lower than Los Angeles and Detroit.

The quality of housing is lower in the area, with 25.8 percent of all housing units classified as not sound (deteriorated or dilapidated) against 10 percent in the remainder of the city.[14] The proportion of housing units sharing bathrooms is almost three times as high as in the remainder of the city (8.9 percent vs. 3.1 percent).

In 1960 there was less living space (in terms of rooms) within the area than in the total city (4.5 rooms per housing unit vs. 5.7). This fact coupled with a higher population per household (3.20 vs. 3.16) results in higher overcrowding rates for the study area (Table 2.8). Approximately 15 percent of all occupied housing units in the area had 1.01 or more persons per room, compared to approximately 6 percent in the remainder of the city. In this characteristic, like many of the others, the whites and non-whites were more alike in the study area than within the total city. The ratio of non-white to white overcrowding rates (proportion of housing units having 1.01 and above persons per room) was 2.33 in the area and 10.00 in the remainder of the city.

TABLE 2.8. PERSONS PER ROOM (AS PERCENT OF TOTAL OCCUPIED
DWELLING UNITS) BY RACE FOR STUDY AND REMAINDER
OF CITY, 1960.

PERSONS/ROOM	WHITE	NON-WHITE	TOTAL
STUDY AREA			
Below 0.5	54.0	38.2	43.4
0.51 - 0.75	18.8	19.7	19.4
0.76 - 1.00	19.0	23.0	21.6
1.01 + over	8.2	19.1	15.5
TOTAL	100.0	100.0	99.9
Total Number of Occ. D.U.	32,730	65,732*	98,462
REMAINDER OF CITY			
Below 0.5	54.6	41.2	50.8
0.51 - 0.75	26.2	20.7	24.6
0.76 - 1.00	17.6	22.0	18.8
1.01 + over	1.6	16.0	5.8
TOTAL	100.0	99.9	100.0
Total Number of Occ. D.U.	368,205	149,100	517,305

Proportion Non-White 1.01 and over.	Study Area	Remainder of City
Proportion White 1.01 and over	2.33	10.0

*The number of non-white dwelling units is lower than the actual number in the area, because only those tracts having over 100 non-white are reported. In the study area there are four non-reported tracts which included a total of approximately 190 non-white units. (Note: The data is compiled by the author.)

V. DELINQUENCY

As can be seen from Table 2.9, the study area can be characterized as a high delinquent area.

TABLE 2.9.   DISTRIBUTION OF STUDY AREA TRACTS WITHIN QUINTILE
DISTRIBUTION OF PHILADELPHIA TRACTS (378) FOR
JUVENILE (ages 7-17) CONTACTS[1] WITH POLICE, 1960.

QUINTILE NUMBER	CONTACT RATE[2]	NUMBER OF STUDY AREA TRACTS	% OF CITY[2,3]	% OF STUDY AREA TRACTS
1	0.0 - 2.4	3	3.9	7.3
2	2.5 - 4.2	0	0.0	0.0
3	4.3 - 7.3	4	5.3	9.8
4	7.4 - 12	12	15.8	29.3
5	12 and above	22	28.9	53.6
TOTAL		41	10.9	100.0

[1]Each juvenile is counted once, regardless of the number of contacts.

[2]Rate is based on residence of offender.

[3]Since the exact number of city tracts within each quintile was not given, it was assumed that each quintile contained 76 tracts, which would sum to 380 tracts.

NOTE: The original source of this data is supplied by the Philadelphia, Police Department, Research and Planning Division.

According to official Philadelphia Police statistics the area contributes more than its share to the two highest quintiles; approximately 83% of the census tracts in the area (in terms of police rates). In fact, over one-half of the tracts in the area are concentrated in the highest city quintile. The conclusion is the same, according to an independent city-wide study conducted for the same time period. Stanley H. Turner[15] reports a delinquency rate in the area 2.3 times as high as the remainder of the city (11.1 juvenile offenders per 1,000 persons vs. 4.9).

VI. CONCLUSION

The study area, in comparison to the total city, is, among other things, low in family income, high in the proportion of low prestige jobs, low educational level, low rate of owner-occupancy, larger average household size and higher rates of room overcrowding. All of these variables have been found to be significant variables in accounting for the spatial distribution of delinquents.[16] To what extent these or similar factors will be successful in distinguishing between the delinquent and non-delinquent in a high delinquent area is a matter still to be determined.

Footnotes:

1. Much of the discussion in this chapter is based on <u>Fact Book for North Philadelphia</u>, Philadelphia Council for Community Advancement, 1964, unless otherwise noted. This document was prepared by the staff of the Sociology Department, Temple University, under the supervision of Holger Stub, and almost all of the 1960 census data utilized in the report is from: United States Bureau of Census, <u>U.S. Census of Population and Housing, 1960, Census Tracts, Philadelphia</u>, Final Report PHC (1), 116, United States Government Printing Office, Washington, D.C., 1962.

2. For the geographic boundaries of the area, see Appendix, p. 123.

3. The index is defined in the following manner: If N_i represents the proportion of Negroes in the city residing in the ith tract and W_i, the proportion of whites in the city residing in the ith tract, then the segregation index (S.I.) is defined as:

$$\frac{\sum_{i=1}^{k} W_i - N_i}{2} \times 100$$

The S.I. can take any value between 0 and 100 and can be interpreted to mean the percent of Negroes (or vice versa) who would have to move to equal the percent distribution of whites. Thus, a S.I. of 90, computed on the basis of census tracts, means that 90 percent of the Negroes must move into other tracts to equalize the distribution of white and Negro <u>between tracts,</u> i.e., W_i and N_i must both have the same value in all tracts. It must be emphasized that the proportion of whites and Negroes within tracts would not be equal, but only be in the same ratio as in the city. In addition, tracts may be equalized (S.I. = 0), but segregation can still continue within tracts, namely segregated blocks. Therefore, one may obtain a much different result by computing S.I. on the basis of blocks instead of census tracts. For a general discussion of segregation indices and similar measures, see Otis Dudley Duncan and Beverly Duncan, "A Methodological Analysis of Segregation Indexes", <u>American Sociological Review</u>, 20 (April, 1955), pp. 210-217. For an example of a specific application, see their "Residential Distribution and Occupational Stratification", <u>American Journal of Sociology</u>, 60 (March, 1955), pp. 493-503.

4. The segregation indices for the city were obtained from Jerome Melamed, "Negro Residential Segregation in Philadelphia, 1950 - 1960", Unpublished graduate paper, Temple University, 1966. The S.I.'s for the study area were computed by the author.

    In computing the S.I. over time, the problem of changing tract boundaries has to be faced. The changes in the study area from 1950 to 1960 were quite extensive, with only 56 percent of the 1960 tracts having the same boundaries as in 1950. Fortunately, almost all of the changes were within the external boundaries of the area, which means that the 1960 area can be reconstructed for 1950 without much difficulty. There were only portions of two 1950 tracts (38B and 38E) that were not included in the study area in 1960. They contained 5,202 whites and 323 Negroes, representing about 2 percent of the 1950 area white population and 0.2 percent of the Negroes. In order to decide what proportion of each of the two tracts to utilize for the 1950 data, the 1960 tracts, to which portions of the two tracts were assigned, were checked for relative growth from 1950 to 1960. One 1960 tract (containing part of the 1950 38B) seemed somewhat stable; thus, one-half (112 whites and 152 Negroes) of the population in 38B was assigned to the study area. All of the persons (4,978 whites and 19 Negroes) in 38E were assigned to the study area, since the corresponding 1960 tract grew by more than 50 percent from 1950 to 1960. The 1940 to 1950 period presented no problem since 92 percent of the census tracts were unchanged since 1940, and the external boundaries of the area were the same in 1940 and 1950.

The change of tract boundaries within the area may still affect the S.I. however. The assumption has to be made that the boundary changes in no way affected the relative distribution of whites and Negroes between tracts, i.e., the S.I. can be affected by simply manipulating boundaries in such a manner as to minimize or maximize the dispersion of one population within another. How tenable is this assumption? There is no direct test, but it is possible that the assumption is a bad one. If, in the determination of tract boundaries, the decision is to minimize heterogeneity within tracts, and if racial characteristics is one of the variables entering into this administrative decision, then it is possible that the S.I. is somewhat inflated.

5. See Karl E. Taeuber and Alma F. Taeuber, "The Negro as an Immigrant Group: Recent Trends in Racial and Ethnic Segregation in Chicago", American Journal of Sociology, 69 (January, 1964), pp. 374-382.

6. These figures were supplied by Stanley H. Turner from his own research. The square mileage for tracts was obtained by Turner from the Philadelphia Planning Commission. The total square miles in the area was 9.88, representing 7.6 percent of the city.

7. The figures cited here are those of the census and are only true for the week of the enumeration. The long-term or yearly averages might lead to somewhat different figures.

8. The occupational categories in Table 2.3 are shorthand labels for the usual census categories: Professional, technical and kindred workers; managers, officials and proprietors, including farm; clerical and kindred workers; sales; craftsmen, foremen and kindred workers; operatives and kindred workers; private household; service, except mine workers.

9. High prestige jobs are defined as professional, managerial, clerical, sales, and craftsmen and foremen; low prestige jobs are operatives, private household, service, laborer, and unreported occupations. This division basically reflects the traditional white-blue collar dichotomy, with the one exception of including skilled workers and foremen in the white collar category. (The assumption is that the skilled workers, in terms of income, life style and prestige, are more akin to white collar than blue collar. See Kurt Mayer, Class and Society, Revised Edition, New York: Random House, 1955, p. 47.)

10. It must be realized that from 1950 to 1960 the city as a whole experienced a decline in the labor force, resulting in a loss of practically all job classifications. Consequently, the discussion is really concerned with which categories are losing (in an absolute sense) at a faster or slower rate than the total city.

11. These classifications represent employed males only. Since there were approximately 10,000 males 14 years and over in the area (most of them non-whites) who were not employed in the 1960 survey, it is possible that the up-grading of the non-white occupational structure that was noted above is misleading. If most of those 10,000 males were in the low prestige classifications, then the picture may be reversed.

12. Who these professionals are I cannot say without further evidence. The professionals in the city may include the increasing number of non-white teachers, but more interesting is the phenomenon of white professionals within the study area who obviously could not be non-white teachers and probably are not even teachers.

13. Of the 920 Negro youths in the sample in this study, 65.8 percent came from households headed by a male, 27.9 percent by a female. In 6.0 percent of the cases there was disagreement between the adult and the youth, and 0.3 percent were unknown. Remember that the base figures are youths and not households. Since some of the boys came from the same household, the above percentages would be slightly different. In addition, these figures are not the same as "broken home" rates, since some of these youths were living with their father only, or guardian of one sort or another.

14. The base for computing ownership rates differs from that for quality of housing. In the former, the base is occupied units, whereas in the latter it is total housing units. Since, in all likelihood, a good portion of the vacant units are substandard, the quality of the occupied units is probably better than the figure cited above would indicate. If we assume that all 7,962 vacant units in the area were substandard, then the minimum substandard rate based on occupied units would be 19.7 percent; doing the same for the remainder of the city, the rate would be 7.2 percent. Consequently, even if all the vacant units in the city were substandard (and they probably are not), the gap would still exist.

15. From on-going research. Data on offenders was drawn from a larger study (see Thorsten Sellin and Marvin Wolfgang, Measurement of Delinquency, New York: J. Wiley and Sons, 1964) based on a 10 percent sample of all offenses known to Philadelphia police in 1960 which (1) had any juvenile offender, and (2) resulted in physical injury or property damage or loss.

16. William M. Bates, The Ecology of Juvenile Delinquency in St. Louis, unpublished Ph.D. dissertation, Washington University, St. Louis, Mo., 1959 (portions reported in his "Caste, Class and Vandalism", Social Problems, 9 (Spring, 1962), pp. 349-353; D.J. Bordua, "Juvenile Delinquency and Anomie", Social Problems, 6 (Winter, 1958), pp. 230-238; Ronald J. Chilton, Social Factors and the Residential Distribution of Official Delinquents, Indianapolis, Indiana, unpublished Ph.D. dissertation, Indiana University, Bloomington, Inc., 1962 (portions reported

in his "Continuities in Delinquency and Research", American Sociological Review, 29 (February, 1964), pp. 71-83; James J. Conlin, <u>An Area Study of Juvenile Delinquency in Baltimore, Maryland</u>, unpublished Ph.D. dissertation, St. Louis University, St. Louis, Mo., 1961; Maurice F. Connery, <u>An Ecological Study of Juvenile Delinquency in St. Paul,</u> unpublished Ph.D. dissertation, Columbia University, New York, N. Y., 1960; Bernard Lander, <u>Towards an Understanding of Juvenile Delinquency</u>, New York, Columbia University Press, 1954.

For a general methodological criticism of these studies, see Kenneth Polk, "Urban Social Areas and Delinquency", <u>Social Problems</u>, 14 (1967), pp. 320-324; Lawrence Rosen and Stanley H. Turner, "An Evaluation of the Lander Approach to Ecology of Delinquency", <u>Social Problems</u>, 15 (Fall, 1967), pp. 189-200; Robert A. Gordon, "Issues in the Ecological Study of Delinquency", <u>American Sociological Review</u>, 32 (December, 1967), pp. 927-944.

CHAPTER THREE

FAMILY STRUCTURE

The family suggests itself as an important factor in delinquency primarily because it is often viewed as a "basic" and "primary" socializing
agent. The reasoning employed in tracing out the relationship between delinquency and family is fairly simple: If the family has primary relevance
for the development of "conforming" behavior, and if delinquency represents
"non-conforming" behavior, then it is likely that the family is somehow an
important factor in explaining that non-conformity. However the failure of
the family in this regard may occur along several lines:

(1) "Deviant Structure". An ideal or model structure is postulated
     (usually the most frequently occuring type in the society) and
     any deviation from this ideal structure is viewed as "bad" and
     producing "bad" consequences (such as delinquency).[1] In Ameri-
     can society the structurally ideal family is the nuclear family
     with both natural parents present. The "broken" (or deviant)
     family may result in an inability for the remaining parent or
     parent surrogates to "control" the child, fail to act as proper
     "role-models", or fail to contribute sufficient maternal or
     paternal love.

(2) Deviant family relationships. The assumption is that a certain
     ideal "quality" of parent-child, sibling-sibling, or husband-
     wife relationship will more likely result in conforming or
     "well-adjusted" behavior. Thus, lack of love or too much love,
     an unhappy home, a too harsh or too lax father, an authoritarian
     or permissive parent, lack of family solidarity, parental in-
     consistency, etc. are seen as resulting in rebellion, personal-
     ity problems, defective "generalized other", etc. with resultant
     increased probability of delinquency.

(3) Transfer of "Deviant" norms. A "normal" or non-pathological
     socialization process is assumed, and instead, the difference
     between delinquents and non-delinquents resides in the content
     of the norms internalized by the youths during socialization
     within the family. In other words, delinquents had been taught
     norms and values, by family members, which would favor the vio-
     lation of juvenile statutes, and the non-delinquent has acquired
     norms and values which are unfavorable to violation of laws (in
     the Sutherland "differential association" sense). In this con-
     text one investigates the nature and content of the norms taught
     rather than the nature of the socialization process.

Of course, these are not always viewed as independent dimensions (e.g.,
a "broken home" may lead to "defective" family relationships), however, they
probably represent the three major ways in which the family is used to explain delinquency.

Although contemporary sociologists tend to concentrate on non-familial variables (peer group, subculture, gang, social structure, opportunity structure, etc.),[2] the family seems to be the most popular "cause" of delinquency accepted by the public.[3]

The primary concern of this chapter is to ascertain the degree to which various aspects of "deviant family structure" can distinguish the delinquent from the non-delinquent. There are four major factors analyzed in this chapter: (1) absence or presence of parents, (2) matriarchy, (3) ordinal position and (4) household size. The analysis in Chapter Two has shown that the study area, in relation to the total city, has a larger average household size and a larger proportion of persons under 18 not living with both parents. No specific census information was available to evaluate the frequency of female dominated households, but there is a fair amount of certainty that the area does have a larger proportion of such households. There was no data, as well, for ordinal position in the area, however the larger average family size in the area would result in a larger proportion of intermediate children and a smaller number of only, youngest and eldest children.

I. ABSENCE AND PRESENCE OF PARENTS

Much has been written and researched about the "broken home" and delinquency, and perhaps it remains one of the seemingly more obvious and "facile" single causes of delinquency. However before discussing the adequacy of the concept as a factor in delinquency it will be important to closely examine the concept itself.

Robert Bell speaks about "altered families" and presents a classification system which involves two dimensions: (1) Whether or not the "break" is voluntary, and (2) Whether or not the reason for the break is internal to the family.[4] Within this schema Bell includes situations where the parents or parent are physically absent, and also where the parent is present but unable to perform his or her parental role because of illness or some other personal reason. (This may well be called "functionally absent" to contrast with the condition of "physically absent".) For purposes of this study it seemed expedient to modify the Bell schema and refer only to physical absence of the parent or parents.[5] The resulting typology can be represented in the following manner:

	Voluntary	Involuntary
External	I	II
Internal	III	IV

Type I, the external-voluntary, includes those cases in which there are temporary dislocations, primarily the consequence of the husband's occupation (e.g., traveling salesman, military volunteers, merchant sailor). This type of family is considered to be legally in tact. Type II, external-involuntary, involves institutionalization (hospital, prison, etc.) and military draft. In many cases it is a temporary dislocation and legally once more the family is in tact. The classic family problems of desertion, separation and divorce are incorporated in Type III, internal-voluntary. It is perhaps best also to include in Type III, families which never began, namely, a mother with illegitimate children. The break in Type III tends to be longer or in some cases permanent. Finally, death is the only case in Type IV, internal-involuntary, and of course the break is permanent and legally the marriage no longer exists.

Each of the four types may have varying degrees of importance for male delinquency. Types III and IV would have the longest time for absence of a parent or parents, Type II less, and Type I the least. If delinquency is associated with duration of absence of a parent or parents one would expect Type III and IV to have the highest rates of delinquency, Type II the next lowest and the lowest for Type I. If strain and conflict in the family is of paramount importance, then Type III should exhibit the highest rates of delinquency. (Keep in mind this is only with respect to other types of altered families, and not in comparison with intact families. As will be discussed below, there is some debate that conflict and tension, or adjustment to same, is less likely to occur in an intact family than in one broken by divorce, desertion or separation.)

The "broken family" is almost always defined as one or both natural parents absent because of death, desertion, divorce or separation. Thus, in terms of the typology presented above, Types III and IV are the altered families usually considered in studies of delinquency. However, as will be seen below, this concept of "broken home" cannot be used with complete certainty in this study.

The literature in delinquency and criminology exhibits a fair amount of controversy on the issue of importance of "broken home" for male delinquency. The arguments have ranged from one extreme to another. For example, Peterson and Becker strongly support the variable when they state that:

> .....the substantial relationship between delinquency and broken
> homes remains as one of the overriding facts any conception of de-
> linquency must take into account.[6]

On the other hand, there is the biting criticism by Mannheim:

> No other term in the history of criminological thought has been
> so much overworked, misused, and discredited as this. For many
> years universally proclaimed as the most obvious explanation of
> both juvenile delinquency and adult crime, it is now often re-
> garded as the 'black sheep' in the otherwise respectable family
> of criminological theories, and most writers shamefacedly turn
> their backs to it.[7]

One pair of authors argue that "broken homes" are especially critical in lower-class Negro neighborhoods.

> When linked with the factor of segregation in highly deteri-
> orated neighborhoods, the factor of family disorganization
> among Negroes undoubtedly assumes greater weight in delin-
> quency.[8]

It seems, however, that most criminologists consider the "broken home" concept of secondary importance for delinquency.[9] The two most frequent criticisms of the concept given in the literature are: (1) it is unscientific because it includes too many dimensions (nature of the break, age of the break, attitude toward the break and subsequent adjustments to the break),[10] and (2) it has included only structural characteristics and not the more important dimension of family interaction. Those supporting the second criticism argue that delinquency-producing interactions are as likely to occur in "broken" as "non-broken" homes.[11] (The "quality of interaction" cannot be tested in this study since family "interaction" variables were not part of the design.)

Jackson Toby, in his reexamination of the Shaw and McKay data, argues that broken home is important for younger males only.[12] Toby reaches this conclusion by apparently a simple inspection of the differences in percentage of "broken homes" between delinquents and non-delinquents for each age group. There are several things wrong with this procedure. For one, Toby has percentaged in the wrong direction, he should have looked at the percentage of delinquents within "broken homes" and intact homes.[13] Secondly, the marginals are extremely skewed. For the youngest age group, 10 years old, which had the largest percentage difference for "broken homes", included only twelve delinquents, compared to 1387 non-delinquents. (For 11 year olds there were 55 delinquents and 1409 non-delinquents.) Statements about percentage differences involving such large discrepancies in sample size should be made with extreme caution, if made at all. Finally, percentage differences are poor indices of the size of the difference between two groups. A computation of Tau b for the 10-13 year olds yields a value of 0.006 as compared with 0.004 for the total sample. Consequently, although Toby's statement about younger boys may be technically correct, the differential effect of age on the relationship between "broken home" and delinquency is extremely weak.

What empirical evidence is there for a relationship between "broken home"? In order to make sure "adequate" comparisons with the results of the present study, only those studies were selected for review which met the following criteria:

1. The sample included only male youths or the data was presented in such a manner as to allow the males to be selected out;

2. a control group of non-delinquents (however defined) was part of the research design;

3. the delinquent group did not consist of institutionalized youth only;[14]

4. the data was presented in sufficient detail to enable a Tau b to be computed.

The only study included for analysis which did not meet all of the above criteria was that of the Cluecks; they used an institutionalized population for their sample of delinquents. However, since the study has been cited widely, it was felt that it should be included. In order to make statements about the "strength of the relationship" between "broken home" and delinquency, and thus have a more adequate basis for comparison than just the presence or absence of an association, a Tau b was computed for each study. The ten studies chosen are listed in Table 3.1 in chronological order (by date of publication). The times of the studies vary from 1929 to 1965, and the definition of delinquency varies (official court record, self-reported and "gang" membership).

Despite this variation and although almost all report "significant differences", the conclusion is fairly clear; the strength of the relationship is small. The two studies which report somewhat higher degrees of association are the Gluecks and Browning. The Gluecks' study, as mentioned previously, used an institutional population for its delinquents and thus may include the administrative biases of differential commitment of youths from "broken homes". A second possible reason for the fairly high association is that there is an equal number of delinquents and non-delinquents (because of the "matching" design). Tau b is affected by the marginals in such a manner that its value is maximized when there is a 50-50 split in the marginals.[15] Reordering of the Gluecks' data to give a split of 30% delinquents and 70% non-delinquents (which is somewhat comparable to the proportion of delinquents in this study) yields a Tau b of .018 (still significant at the .001 level). The Browning study seemed to employ the least systematic sampling procedure of all the studies consulted. The non-delinquents were not selected on a probability basis, and the delinquents chosen were only those who had either committed a truancy (to represent a non-serious offense) or auto theft (to represent a serious offense). The weakness of the sample is reflected in the fairly high proportion of delinquents (66.5%).

None of the studies in Table 3.1 were interested in the universe of youths residing in high-Negro, high delinquency areas, with the possible exception of the Tennyson study. The control group in the Tennyson study was lower-class Negro boys,[16] and it reported almost no association between "broken home" and "gang" membership. An interesting aspect of this study is that the definition of "broken home" included the dimension of time, i.e., an attempt was made to include only those "breaks" which had some duration in time.[17] One implication which might be gleaned from Tennyson's result is that the time of the "break" has little impact on subsequent delinquency. However, such a conclusion should be held with caution. For one, the determination of the time of the "break" was extremely imprecise; secondly, the sampling of non-gang members was non-systematic and, thirdly, delinquency was not "official delinquency" but only membership in a "troublesome" gang.

The reliable information on the ecological importance of broken home is limited. Barker in his study in Chicago (no date given) concludes that "broken home" is insufficient to account for the spatial distribution of delinquents.[18] However he reaches this conclusion in a somewhat questionable manner. Instead of utilizing the more conventional procedure of correlating delinquency rates with rates of "broken home", the author correlated the proportion of delinquents coming from homes where parents were divorced with the proportion of delinquents coming from intact homes, and the proportion of delinquents coming from homes where the parents were separated or one had deserted with the proportion of delinquents coming from intact homes. The correlation values were quite high (0.79 and 0.78 respectively), hence the conclusion that delinquents were as likely to come from areas characterized by high "broken home" rates as from areas of low rates. The potential error lies in the fact that the two variables in question are not completely independent; there is a partial mathematical dependence between them. In both correlations the two rates being correlated have the same base, total number of delinquents. Simply on the basis of the partial mathematical dependence between the two rates for each correlation, one could expect high correlation values. Consequently the author's conclusion of no relationship between "broken home" and delinquency, must be viewed with something less than full confidence.

Shaw and Mckay report a product moment r of 0.19 (not significant) between rates of broken homes in 29 schools in Chicago and the delinquency rates in the areas in which the schools are located.[19] In contrast, Weeks and Smith report a significant r value of 0.38 between the delinquency rates and "broken home" rates on 32 school districts in Spokane.[20] Finally, Connery's ecological study of St. Paul found a correlation of 0.62 (significant) between delinquency rates and the proportion of persons, 14 and over, widowed and divorced.[21] This, of course, is not the same as "broken home" but there is probably some overlap. To sum, the ecological findings for "broken home" are mixed.

As part of the interview schedules used in this study, the youth was asked to list all persons living in the household. The information requested for each person was: Relationship to the respondent, sex, age, education, kind of work, if the mother works, and in the case of missing parents, if they are dead or alive. In addition, the respondents were asked to indicate who was the "main wage earner" was. The adult respondents listed all persons over 18 living in the household, along with relationship, age, sex, kind of work and who was the "main wage earner". By consulting the responses on this question (who is present) for both youth and adult it is possible to determine if both parents were physically present at the time of the interview. Several bits of information were <u>not</u> collected, e.g.: reason for absence and, in the case of a dead parent, if the death occurred before or after leaving the household. In addition, there was no systematic attempt to determine if the parent or parents listed were step-parents. The loss of this information has some very important consequences:

1. There is no way to determine if the absence of parent or parents occurred before or after the acquisition of a J.A.D. record for the youth. Thus, no definitive statement can be made about direction of causality.

2. Since the reason for the absence is not known, it is impossible to formally use the classic notion of "broken home". There is no way of knowing if the family is Type I, II or III. (The suspicion is that the probability of Type I is small since parents temporarily absent because of occupation would in all likelihood be considered as "living" in the household, especially if he or she is listed as the "main wage earner". However, this is not known with any certainty.)

3. In cases where the missing parent was dead, it was not known if death was the cause of the break which means that there is no way of distinguishing between Type III or IV family.

In sum, the variable which will be utilized in this study will be absence of parent or parents (either natural or step) at the time of the interview, or here after referred to as "altered family".

The separate listing of household members by the adult allowed for a reliability check on the responses of the youth. As can be expected, there were some disagreements on the presence or absence of parent or parents. In all there were a total of 57 cases (6.2% of the total sample) where a discrepancy between youth and adult existed. The nature of the disagreements are listed in Table 3.2.

TABLE 3.1.   SUMMARY OF STUDIES INVESTIGATING "BROKEN
HOME" AND DELINQUENCY.

RESEARCHER	YEAR PUBLISHED	N	ASSOCIATION Tau b	Chi^2 (1)
Shaw and McKay[2]	1932	8953	.004	40.28
Weeks and Smith[3]	1939	2449	.012	24.49
Carr-Saunders, et al[4]	1944	1925	.019	39.25
Glueck and Glueck[5]	1950	1000	.078	78.50
Nye[6]	1958	1160	.005	5.80
Browning[7]	1960	164	.096	15.69
Hardt[8]	1965	164	.022	3.66
Hardt[9]	1965	191	.015	2.92
Tennyson[10]	1967	294	<.001	.06
Koval and Polk[11]	1967	819	.009	7.81

[1]All Chi Square values are for one degree of freedom. Significant values are: For .001 level, 10.83; for 0.1 level, 6.64; and
for .05 level, 3.84.

[2]Clifford Shaw and H. D. McKay, "Are Broken Homes a Causative
factor in Juvenile Delinquency?" Social Forces, 10 (May, 1932),
pp. 514-524. Delinquents are from Juvenile Court in Chicago, 1929-
1930. The non-delinquents, ages 10-17, were sampled from public
schools in Chicago. The delinquency status of the control group
was not checked; therefore, it is not known how many delinquents
were in the control group. They included "prolonged absence due
to confinement in an institution" in their definition of "broken
home".

[3]H. A. Weeks and Margaret G. Smith, "Juvenile Delinquency
and Broken Homes in Spokane, Washington", Social Forces, 18
(October, 1939), pp. 48-59. Delinquents are from Juvenile Court
in Spokane, Washington. The non-delinquents are a random sample
of public secondary school students, Spokane, Washington, 1937,
having no court record. The age of delinquency is from 7-18.

[4]A. M. Carr-Saunders, H. Mannheim and E. Rhodes, Young
Offenders, New York: MacMillan, 1944. Delinquents (ages 7-17)
are taken from those appearing before court in 1938 in selected
cities in England (including London). The non-delinquents were
chosen by asking the head teacher at the school at which the

delinquent attended for a youth who would be similar to the delinquent youth.   The matching variables were age and residence.

[5]Sheldon Glueck and Eleanor Glueck, Unraveling Juvenile Delinquency, New York: Commonwealth Fund, 1950.   The sample of delinquents was taken from "correctional schools" and the non-delinquents from Boston public schools in 1939.   The delinquents
and non-delinquents were matched for age, ethnic origin and in-
telligence.

[6]F. Ivan Nye, Family Relationships and Delinquent Behavior,
New York: John Wiley and Sons, 1958.   The sample was selected from
high school students in three "medium-sized" towns in Washington
in 1955.   The measurement of delinquency was that of "self-reporting", with the delinquent group being those scoring highest
on the delinquency scale.   The association values noted include
step-parents in the intact family; a reconstruction of the broken
home definition to include step-parents yields a Tau b of less
than .001 and Chi^2 of 1.16.

[7]Charles J. Browning, "Differential Impact of Family Disorganization on Male Adolescents", Social Problems, 8 (Summer,
1960), pp. 37-44.   The youths were chosen from a population
that was white, at least third generation Americans, Protes-
tant, Catholic or no religion, enrolled in public schools, and
living in a common court jurisdiction within Los Angeles.   (No
date given) The mean age of the youths in the sample was 15.
The delinquents were defined as those having a court record and
whose most serious offense was auto theft or truancy (the analysis divided delinquency into most serious and least serious).
The non-delinquents were those who had no record of truancy for
the year of the study.   The proportion of delinquents was 66.5%.

[8]Robert H. Hardt, "Delinquency and Social Class: Studies of
Juvenile Deviations or Police Dispositions", unpublished paper
presented at Eastern Sociological Meetings, New York, 1965.   The
study was conducted in 1963 in a city of 250,000 located in "the
center of one of the major metropolitan areas in a Middle Atlantic
state".   Delinquents were defined as having a record or a "sus-
pected" or "alledged" delinquent in the Central Registry of Juvenile Police Contacts.   Both the delinquents and non-delinquents
were seventh, eighth and ninth grade students attending parochial
and public schools.

[9]Ibid.   The sample is the same as noted above (note 8) except
that delinquency was defined as self-report.

[10]Ray A. Tennyson, "Family Structure and Delinquent Behavior"
in Malcolm W. Klein (Editor), Juvenile Gangs in Context, Englewood Cliffs, New Jersey, Prentice-Hall, 1967, pp. 57-69.   Delinquency was membership in a gang defined as "troublesome" by the

TABLE 3.1.   SUMMARY OF STUDIES INVESTIGATING "BROKEN
HOME" AND DELINQUENCY.   (Cont'd)

"Program for Detached Workers of the YMCA of Chicago".   The non-
gang members were lower-class Negro boys.   (This sample was not
a random one.)   The non-gang members were suggested by the YMCA
workers.   An intact home was a response by the youth of either
"Both parents continuously" or "mostly both parents" to the question, "Whom did you live with when growing up?"

[11]John P. Koval and Kenneth Polk, "Problem Youth in a Small
City", in Malcolm W. Klein (Editor), Juvenile Gangs in Context,
Englewood Cliffs, New Jersey, Prentice-Hall, 1967, pp. 123-138.
Sample taken from one high school (N=815) and a non-probability
selection of "drop-outs" (N=53) residing in a "small city" in
Lane County, Oregon (no date given).   Delinquency was defined
as a court or police record, with family structure being charac-
terized only as "natural family intact".

TABLE 3.2. AGREEMENTS AND DISAGREEMENTS BETWEEN YOUTH AND ADULT RESPONDENTS CONCERNING PRESENCE OF PARENT OR PARENTS.

	N	%
Agreements	864	93.8
Adult says father present, youth says absent	13	93.8
Youth says father present, adult says absent	38	1.4
Adult says mother present, youth says absent	4	0.4
Youth says mother present, adult says absent	1	0.1
Other	1	0.1
Total disagreements	(57)	(6.2)
Total	921	100.0

The large bulk of disagreements concern the father, and most of these consist of the youth reporting the father present while the adult reported him absent.

Some possible reasons for the disagreements are:

1. A youth not wanting to admit the absence of his father;
2. a paramour was identified as a parent by the youth or the adult, but not both;
3. a wife disclaiming the presence of a husband because she fears the loss of public welfare;
4. youth not clearly perceiving a break, especially if it had recently occurred;
5. the interviewer's question being misunderstood by one of the respondents.

There was no way of determining which reason or reasons may have been the important ones. Since there is no reliable way of evaluating what these disagreements represented they were omitted from any analysis involving altered family.[22]

The results for the altered family variables are presented in Table 3.3. There are differences between altered and intact families and in the expected direction. The largest association reported is for definition I (presence of and J.A.D. record) with 45.0% of the altered family youths having a J.A.D. record and 35.7% from intact families possessing no such record. However, even though this difference is significant (at the .01 level), the variability accounted for is small (1.2%). Thus, the variable in specifying delinquents in this sample.

It may be argued that "breaks" due to separation, divorce or desertion may

44

have greater consequence for delinquency than breaks due to death.[23] Sterne reports no significant differences in seriousness of offense committed and type of break (death vs. not death) for his sample of juvenile delinquents.[24] To what extent is death of missing parent associated with delinquency in this study? This question is evaluated in Table 3.4.

TABLE 3.3. DELINQUENCY STATUS (AS MEASURED BY THREE DE-
FINITIONS OF DELINQUENCY) BY PRESENCE OR AB-
SENCE OF PARENTS IN YOUTH'S FAMILY.

TYPE OF FAMILY	DEFINITION OF DELINQUENCY					
	I^1		II^2		III^3	
	J.D.	NON J.D.	J.D.	NON J.D.	J.D.	NON J.D.
Altered[4] (N=344)						
n	155	189	97	247	128	216
%	45.0	55.0	28.2	71.8	37.2	62.8
Intact[5] (N=522)						
n	181	341	104	418	143	379
%	34.7	65.3	19.9	80.1	27.4	72.6
Total (N=866) *						
n	336	530	201	665	271	595
%	38.8	61.2	23.2	76.8	31.3	68.7
Tau b	.012		.009		.011	
Chi^2	10.13		7.88		9.27	
Pr. Interval	.001 to .01		.001 to .01		.001 to .01	

[1]J.A.D. record, any offense.

[2]Offense against property or person as most serious offense on J.A.D. record.

[3]J.A.D. record, excluding juvenile status offense as most serious offense.

[4]At least one parent absent.

[5]Both parents absent.

*Excludes 55 cases in which there was a disagreement between adult and youth on the presence of parents.

Source: Appendix, Table 1.

45

TABLE 3.4.   DELINQUENCY STATUS (AS MEASURED BY THREE
             DEFINITIONS OF DELINQUENCY) BY STATUS OF
             MISSING PARENT OR PARENTS.

DEFINITION OF DELINQUENCY[1]

STATUS OF MISSING PARENT	I		II		III	
	J.D.	NON-J.D.	J.D.	NON-J.D.	J.D.	NON-J.D.
One or both alive[2] (N=231)						
n	108	123	66	165	89	142
%	46.8	53.2	28.6	71.4	38.5	61.5
One or both dead (N=86)						
n	38	48	25	61	32	54
%	44.2	55.8	29.1	70.9	37.2	62.8
Total (N=317)*						
n	146	171	91	226	121	196
%	46.1	53.9	28.7	71.3	38.2	61.8
Tau b	.002		<.001		<.001	
Chi[2]	0.60		0.03		0.03	
Pr. Interval	.30 to .50		.80 to .90		.80 to .90	

[1]The three definitions are the same as given in Table 3.3.

[2]In the case of two missing parents the youth was included
 in this category only if both parents were alive, otherwise he was placed in the other category.

*Excludes 27 cases where the status of the missing parent
 or parents could not be determined.

Source: Appendix, Table 2.

The youths of altered families are divided into two groups: (1) the missing parent is alive, and (2) the missing parent is dead. In the case where both parents were missing, the cause of the break was considered to be death if at least one parent was dead. An inspection of Table 3.4 indicates that there is no significant relationship for all three definitions of delinquency. As noted previously, since it is not known when the death occurred, it is not certain that death was the reason for the break. The only certainty that exists is that death was not the cause of the family alteration in the cases of absent and living parents.

To conclude, in the light of the limitations (as discussed above) of the "altered family" definition used in this study, it is quite conceivable that the reason for the small association of delinquency and altered family is the "unscientific" nature of the concept (i.e., it masks many important dimensions), although on the one dimension investigated, death vs. non-death, no important differences were noted. In any case "broken home" (or in the case of this study, altered family) is in itself not an important factor in distinguishing between a delinquent and non-delinquent in a high delinquent area because, on the basis of available evidence (see Table 3.1) the factor of "broken home" in general is not important.[25]

Before leaving the question of missing parents, the problem of absent mother deserves some attention. Bell[26] has argued that the absence of a mother may be more "serious" than the absence of a father.

> In one respect it may be argued that the man is needed in
> the marriage role for that role relationship to continue
> but that he may be much less needed for the continuation
> of the parent-child role relationship. While the evidence
> is not too strong, it does suggest that the father fills
> primarily a supportive parental role and therefore the
> decreasing significance of the father role often does
> not generally decrease the total parental functions within
> the family.[27]

The available evidence for the effect of an absent mother on delinquency is contradictory. John Bowlby reports among a sample of child guidance center clients in London that a greater proportion of "thieves" had maternal separation during the first five years than "non-thieves".[28] Siri Ness[29] tested the Bowlby hypothesis, which is:

> Prolonged physical separation (that is, a physical separation
> lasting at least three months, probably more than six) of a
> child from his mother (or from the permanent foster mother or
> adoptive mother) during the first five years of life stands
> foremost among the causes of delinquent character development,
> where this expresses itself in delinquent acts like stealing,
> truancy, violent behavior, etc.[30]

He found no support for it with his sample of Oslo youths. Robert G. Andry[31] reports that paternal rejection is more important than maternal rejection. (The Andry study did not employ physical separation as the independent variable, but quality of the parent-child relationship, i.e., the withholding of maternal and paternal love.)

47

Of the studies cited in Table 3.1 only those of Nye and Tennyson reported any findings for mother absent households, however the small number of such cases in both studies (ten for Nye and eight for Tennyson) preclude any substantial conclusion.

The results of this study tend to support Bell's assertion. The percentage of youths having a J.A.D. record was largest (50%) for those who came from homes where the mother was absent.[32] This group also was highest for person crimes and other crimes (excluding property and juvenile status). These differences should be viewed with extreme caution since there were only 20 cases where the mother was the only parent absent.

Even if maternal separation does prove to be associated with delinquency, it is fairly certain that it cannot be considered a salient factor because of the small number of mother-absent families.

II. MATRIARCHY

Within recent years, there has been speculation that the absence of male role models is a critical factor for behavior of lower-class Negro youths.[33] Pettigrew concludes after his survey of relevant research that the absent father is a factor in delinquency, schizophrenia, sexual identification and related problems.[34] W. B. Miller speculates that the "female dominant" household produces a "toughness" response, in lower-class male youths, very often resulting in delinquency, as a reaction to feminine identification.[35]

Among American sociologists Parsons is perhaps the most prominent theorist who has suggested that a strong attachment of a young male to his mother may result in problems for that youth. Although Parsons was concerned with the middle class situation of a father being away from home in pursuit of his occupation, we can extrapolate to the more general situation of the absence of a strong male figure.

> The boy...., has a tendency to form a direct feminine identi-
> fication, since his mother is the model most readily available
> and significant to him. But he is not destined to become an
> adult woman. Moreover, he soon discovers that, since in certain
> vital respects women are considered inferior to men, it would be
> shameful for him to grow up to be like a woman. Hence, when boys
> emerge into what the Freudians call the latency period, their
> behavior tends to be marked by a kind of compulsive masculinity.
> They refuse to have anything to do with girls. To be called
> "sissy" is the worst of all insults. They become interested in
> athletics and physical prowess, in the things in which men have
> the most primitive advantage over women. Furthermore, they be-
> come allergic to all expression of tender emotion; they must be
> "tough". This universal pattern bears all the ear marks of a
> reaction formation. It is the result not simply of masculine
> nature but largely of a defense against a feminine identifica-
> tion.

In addition to the mother being the object of love and identification, she is to the young boy the principal agent of socially
significant discipline. Not only does she administer the disci-
plines which make him a tolerable citizen of the family group, but
she stimulates him to give a good account of himself outside the
home and makes known her disappointment and disapproval if he fails
to measure up to her expectations. She, above all, focuses in her-
self the symbols of what is "good" behavior, of conformity with the
expectations of the respectable adult world. When he revolts against
identification with his mother in the name of masculinity, it is not
surprising that a boy unconsciously identifies goodness with feminin-
ity and that being a "bad boy" becomes a positive goal. It seems
that our association of goodness with femininity--and therewith much
of our ambivalance toward ethical values--has its roots in this situation. At any rate there is a strong tendency for boyish behavior,
in striking contrast to that of preadolescent girls, to run anti-
social if not directly destructive directions.[36]

Despite extensive speculation in this area there has been very little attempt
to test directly the proposition that delinquency is strongly associated with
matriarchy.[37] In perhaps the only empirical evidence on the subject, Tennyson
reports that which parent is dominant has little importance for predicting if
Negro boys join gangs or receive warnings by the police.[38] As mentioned earlier
there is no ecological evidence for matriarchy and delinquency but the apparently
widespread speculation that female dominated households is a prime factor in accounting for delinquency in lower-class Negro areas prompted the inclusion of
the variable in the present study.

The effect of an absent father has already been investigated and found to
be of limited importance.[39] The question still remains if the presence of any
adult males, father or otherwise, is important. An adult male was defined as
any male (including fathers) over eighteen living in the household at the time
of the interview.[40] Although the results are in the expected direction (Table
3.5), the differences in delinquency between the male household and female household are small.

It is possible that the "adult male" variable is too crude; after all,
many different males are involved (uncles, cousins, brothers, etc.) who may have
varying degrees of authority, stability (length of presence) and influence on
the male youth. Bernard, reporting on the unpublished writings of Robert Bell
and Elliot Liebow, argues that the father usually fails to behave in an adequate manner in the father role; therefore, the presence or absence of the father
would have little consequence for delinquency.[41] The implication is that some
other dimension besides presence or absence of males is involved, such as stability, authority or influence.

Four additional variables were used as possible indications of these other
dimensions. They are: (1) sex of household head; (2) sex of main wage earner;
(3) sex of main decision maker; (4) sex of adult who influences the youth most.

The head of the household was defined as the father, if present, and when
absent, the person designated as the main wage earner. This definition was pur-
posely chosen to attempt to approximate the 1960 U.S. census definition of household head:

49

One person in each household is designated as the head, that is,
the person usually living in the structure who is regarded as the
head by the members of the group. However, if a married woman
living with her husband was reported as the head, her husband was
considered as the head for the purposes of simplifying the tabu-
lations.[42]

The definitions differ in that the question of who is the "head" was not asked
in the North Philadelphia Study. The decision maker was defined as the one
whom the youth designated in reply to the question, "What adult in your family
makes most of the family decisions?" The most influential adult was defined as
the one whom the youth designated in reply to the question, "Who in your family
influences you the most?"[43] The main wage earner was whomever the youth so defined. The variables of head of household, main wage earner and main decision
maker were assumed to be indicators of authority figures and the most influential
adult an indicator of "role model" (or significant other").[44]

The findings are given in Tables 3.6 to 3.9. Once more the differences
are small and in the expected direction. Youths from female households (for
all four measures) had higher delinquency rates (for all three definitions).
The findings on the variables of head, main wage earner and decision maker were
significant[45] (with the exception of definition II for decision maker). This
suggests that households having strong "male authority" figures have an effect
of slightly reducing the probability of 13-15 year olds becoming delinquent.

TABLE 3.5. DELINQUENCY STATUS (AS MEASURED BY THREE
            DEFINITIONS OF DELINQUENCY*) BY PRESENCE
            OF ADULT MALES (OVER EIGHTEEN YEARS OF
            AGE) IN HOUSEHOLD OF YOUTH.

DEFINITION OF DELINQUENCY[1]

PRESENCE OF ADULT MALE	I		II		III	
	J.D.	NON-J.D.	J.D.	NON-J.D.	J.D.	NON-J.D.
Yes (N=619)						
n	228	391	138	481	182	437
%	36.8	63.2	22.3	77.6	29.4	70.6
No (N=230)						
n	100	130	55	175	81	149
%	43.5	56.5	23.9	76.1	35.2	64.8
Total (N=849)*						
n	328	521	193	656	263	586
%	38.8	61.2	22.8	77.2	31.0	69.0

Tau b	.004	$<$ .001	.003
Chi^2	3.14	0.25	2.63
Pr. Interval	.05 to .10	.70 to .80	.10 to .20

[1]The three definitions are the same as given in Table 3.3.

*Excludes 72 cases in which there was a disagreement between
 adult and youth on the presence of parents or other adult
 males when father was agreed to be absent.

Source: Appendix, Table 3.

TABLE 3.6. DELINQUENCY STATUS (AS MEASURED BY THREE
            DEFINITIONS OF DELINQUENCY) BY SEX OF
            HOUSEHOLD HEAD.

DEFINITION OF DELINQUENCY[1]

SEX OF HEAD	I		II		III	
	J.D.	NON-J.D.	J.D.	NON-J.D.	J.D.	NON-J.D.
Male (N=606)						
n	219	387	133	473	177	429
%	36.1	63.9	21.9	78.1	29.2	70.8
Female (N-257)						
n	119	138	70	187	96	161
%	46.3	53.7	27.2	72.8	37.4	62.6
Total (N=863)						
n	338	525	203	660	273	590
%	39.2	60.8	23.6	76.3	31.6	68.4

Tau b	.009	.003	.006
Chi^2	7.85	2.76	5.52
Pr. Interval	.001 to .01	.05 to .10	.001 to .02

[1]The three definitions are the same as given in Table 3.3.

*Excludes 3 unknowns and 55 cases in which there were disa-
 greements between adult and youth on the presence of parents.
 (Since the father when present was defined as the head, household head could not be determined in these 55 cases.)

Source: Appendix, Table 4.

TABLE 3.7. DELINQUENCY STATUS (AS MEASURED BY THREE
            DEFINITIONS OF DELINQUENCY) BY SEX OF MAIN
            WAGE EARNER IN YOUTH'S HOUSEHOLD.

DEFINITION OF DELINQUENCY[1]

SEX OF MAIN WAGE EARNER	I		II		III	
	J.D.	NON-J.D.	J.D.	NON-J.D.	J.D.	NON-J.D.
Male (N=578)						
n	202	376	122	456	166	412
%	34.9	65.0	21.1	78.9	28.7	71.3
Female (N=282)						
n	129	153	76	206	100	183
%	45.7	54.3	26.9	73.1	35.5	64.5
Total (N=860)*						
n	331	529	198	662	266	594
%	38.5	61.5	23.1	76.9	30.9	69.1
Tau b	.011		.004		.005	
Chi^2	9.33		3.65		4.02	
Pr. Interval	.001 to .01		.05 to .10		.02 to .05	

[1]The three definitions are the same as given in Table 3.3.

*Excludes 59 unknowns and 2 cases where a male and female
 were named jointly by the youth as main wage earners.

Source: Appendix, Table 5.

TABLE 3.8. DELINQUENCY STATUS (AS MEASURED BY THREE DEFINITIONS OF DELINQUENCY) BY SEX OF MAIN DECISION MAKER IN YOUTH'S HOUSEHOLD.

DEFINITION OF DELINQUENCY[1]

SEX OF DECISION MAKER	I		II		III	
	J.D.	NON-J.D.	J.D.	NON-J.D.	J.D.	NON-J.D.
Male (N=323)						
n	110	213	66	257	91	232
%	30.9	69.1	20.4	79.6	28.2	71.8
Female (N=571)						
n	236	335	137	434	184	387
%	41.3	58.7	24.0	76.0	32.2	67.8
Total (N=894)*						
n	346	548	203	691	275	619
%	38.8	61.2	22.7	77.3	30.8	69.2
Tau b	.010		.002		.008	
Chi^2	8.85		1.43		7.33	
Pr. Interval	.001 to .01		.70 to .80		.001 to .01	

[1]The three definitions are the same as given in Table 3.3.

*Excludes 24 unknowns and 3 cases where a male and female were named jointly by the youth as main decision makers.

Source: Appendix, Table 6.

TABLE 3.9. DELINQUENCY STATUS (AS MEASURED BY THREE
DEFINITIONS OF DELINQUENCY) BY SEX OF ADULT
(LIVING IN HOUSEHOLD OF YOUTH) WHO INFLUENCES
THE YOUTH MOST.

DEFINITION OF DELINQUENCY[1]

SEX OF MOST INF. ADULT	I		II		III	
	J.D.	NON-J.D.	J.D.	NON-J.D.	J.D.	NON-J.D.
Male (N=233)						
n	90	143	45	188	70	163
%	38.6	61.4	19.3	80.7	30.0	70.0
Female (N=682)						
n	266	416	167	515	214	468
%	39.0	61.0	24.5	75.5	31.4	68.6
Total (N=915)*						
n	356	559	212	703	284	631
%	38.9	61.1	23.2	76.8	31.0	69.0
Tau b	< .001		.002		< .001	
Chi^2	0.01		2.13		0.14	
Pr. Interval	.90 to .95		.10 to .20		.90 to .95	

[1]The three definitions are the same as given in Table 3.3.

*Excludes 5 unknowns and 1 case where a male and female
were named jointly by the youth as most influential adult.

Source: Appendix, Table 7.

TABLE 3.10.
DELINQUENCY STATUS (AS MEASURED BY THREE DEFINITIONS OF DELINQUENCY) BY SEX OF MAIN DECISION MAKER IN YOUTH'S HOUSEHOLD FOR INTACT FAMILIES (BOTH PARENTS PRESENT).

DEFINITION OF DELINQUENCY[1]

SEX OF DE-CISION MAKER	I		II		III	
	J.D.	NON-J.D.	J.D.	NON-J.D.	J.D.	NON-J.D.
Male (N=275)						
n	89	186	52	223	75	200
%	32.4	67.6	18.9	81.1	27.3	72.7
Female (N=233)						
n	85	148	46	187	62	171
%	36.5	63.5	19.7	80.3	26.6	73.4
Total (N=508)						
n	174	334	98	410	137	371
%	34.3	65.7	19.3	80.7	27.0	73.0
Tau b	.002		<.001		<.001	
Chi^2	0.94		0.06		0.02	
Pr.Interval	.30 to .50		.80 to .90		.80 to .90	

[1]The three definitions are the same as given in Table 3.3.

Source: Appendix, Table 8.

TABLE 3.11.   DELINQUENCY STATUS (AS MEASURED BY THREE DEFINITIONS
OF DELINQUENCY) BY SEX OF ADULT WHO INFLUENCES THE
YOUTH MOST (LIVING IN YOUTH'S HOUSEHOLD) FOR INTACT
FAMILIES (BOTH PARENTS PRESENT).

DEFINITION OF DELINQUENCY[1]

SEX OF MOST INF. ADULT	I		II		III	
	J.D.	NON-J.D.	J.D.	NON-J.D.	J.D.	NON-J.D.
Male (N=201)						
n	73	128	34	167	56	145
%	36.3	63.7	16.9	83.1	27.9	72.1
Female (N=318)						
n	107	211	70	248	86	232
%	33.6	66.4	22.0	78.0	27.0	73.0
Total (N=519)						
n	180	339	104	415	142	377
%	34.7	65.3	20.1	79.9	27.4	72.6
Tau b	.004		.004		<.001	
Chi^2	2.15		1.99		0.04	
Pr. Interval	.10 to .20		.10 to .20		.80 to .90	

[1]The three definitions are the same as given in Table 3.3.

Source: Appendix, Table 9.

TABLE 3.12.   DELINQUENCY STATUS (AS MEASURED BY THREE DEFINITIONS
OF DELINQUENCY) BY SEX OF HEAD IN YOUTH'S HOUSEHOLD
FOR ALTERED FAMILIES (AT LEAST ONE PARENT ABSENT).

DEFINITION OF DELINQUENCY[1]

SEX OF HEAD	I		II		III	
	J.D.	NON-J.D.	J.D.	NON-J.D.	J.D.	NON-J.D.
Male (N=81)						
n	46	35	26	55	31	50
%	56.8	43.2	32.1	67.9	38.3	61.7
Female (N=256)						
n	118	138	69	187	95	161
%	46.1	53.9	27.0	73.0	37.1	62.9
Total (N=337)						
n	164	173	95	242	126	211
%	48.7	51.3	28.2	71.8	37.4	62.6
Tau b	.008		.002		< .001	
Chi2	2.82		0.80		0.03	
Pr. Interval	.05 to .10		.70 to .80		.70 to .80	

[1]The three definitions are the same as given in Table 3.3.

Source: Appendix, Table 10.

TABLE 3.13.   DELINQUENCY STATUS (AS MEASURED BY THREE
DEFINITIONS OF DELINQUENCY) BY SEX OF MAIN
WAGE EARNER IN YOUTH'S HOUSEHOLD FOR ALTERED
FAMILIES (AT LEAST ONE PARENT ABSENT).

DEFINITION OF DELINQUENCY[1]

SEX OF MAIN WAGE EARNER	I		II		III	
	J.D.	NON-J.D.	J.D.	NON-J.D.	J.D.	NON-J.D.
Male (N=71)						
n	34	37	26	45	30	41
%	47.9	52.1	36.7	63.3	42.2	57.8
Female (N=238)						
n	109	129	63	175	123	115
%	45.8	54.2	26.5	73.5	51.7	48.3
Total (N=309)						
n	143	166	89	220	153	156
%	46.3	53.7	28.8	71.2	49.5	50.5
Tau b	<.001		.001		.006	
Chi^2	0.10		2.74		1.94	
Pr. Interval	.70 to .80		.05 to .10		.10 to .20	

[1]The three definitions are the same as given in Table 3.3.

Source: Appendix, Table 11.

TABLE 3.14.   DELINQUENCY STATUS (AS MEASURED BY THREE
              DEFINITIONS OF DELINQUENCY) BY SEX OF MAIN
              DECISION MAKER IN YOUTH'S HOUSEHOLD FOR
              ALTERED FAMILIES (AT LEAST ONE PARENT ABSENT).

DEFINITION OF DELINQUENCY[1]

SEX OF DECISION MAKER	I		II		III	
	J.D.	NON-J.D.	J.D.	NON-J.D.	J.D.	NON-J.D.
Male (N=39)						
n	16	23	14	25	15	24
%	41.0	59.0	35.9	64.1	38.5	61.5
Female (N=297)						
n	136	161	83	214	112	185
%	45.8	54.2	27.9	72.1	37.7	62.3
Total (N=336)						
n	152	184	97	239	127	209
%	45.3	54.7	28.8	71.2	37.8	62.2
Tau b	.001		.004		<.001	
Chi^2	0.32		1.27		.01	
Pr. Interval	0.50 to 0.70		.20 to .30		.90 to .95	

[1]The three definitions are the same as given in Table 3.3.

Source: Appendix, Table 8.

Quite clearly, the presence or absence of parents determines what "author-ity figures" can possibly be present and might therefore affect the relation-ship with delinquency. Does the sex of an authority figure have any impact on the intact family? The results in Tables 3.10 and 3.11 indicate that the sex of the main decision maker[46] or the most influential person makes very little difference in relationship as to who is delinquent or non-delinquent.[47] The results (Tables 3.12 to 3.14) are much the same for the variables of household head, main wage earner and decision maker for altered families.[48] Although it was impossible to carry out a full partial association analysis for these variables, the available findings indicate that the small but significant associations found for the "authority" variables are due to the general associ-ation of altered family and delinquency reported earlier.

There has been some debate concerning the possible effect of a "strong" female figure for the development of male youths. There are those who argue that the female authority figures produce feminine traits on the young male.[49] (This will be referred to as the feminine identification hypothesis.) The al-ternative argument is that "strong" female authority figures produce an overt, exaggerated masculine reaction to counter the amiguity the youth may feel about his sexuality.[50] (This will be referred to as the masculine protest hypothesis.) The findings to this point indicate that neither argument can be used to ex-plain delinquency in this present sample. It is still possible however, that these notions will be useful in specifying the kind of offense one did commit if he has a J.A.D. record.

Crimes against the person may be viewed as the more "masculine" type of-fenses because they have a greater likelihood of reflecting the masculine be-haviors of aggression and willingness to use physical violence. If a smaller rate of crime against the person for those having a J.A.D. record is found for youths from female households, this would support the feminine identification hypothesis. If the rate for youths from female households is larger, then the masculine protest hypothesis would be supported. The findings (Table 3.15) for three of the four indicators of authority (household head, decision maker and main wage earner) point to the feminine identification hypothesis.

The variable of most influential adult supports the alternative notion. The differences however are not significant for all four indicators.

When a similar analysis is carried out for altered families, (Table 3.16) significant differences are found with the feminine identification hypothesis receiving moderate support. The findings for the main decision maker should be viewed with caution because of the small number (18) of male households. The associations for intact families (Table 3.17) found no significant dif-ferences for the two indicators tested.

TABLE 3.15.   RELATIVE FREQUENCY OF DELINQUENTS HAVING A PERSON
              CRIME AS MOST SERIOUS OFFENSE ON THEIR J.A.D.
              RECORD BY TYPE OF HOUSEHOLD FOR DIFFERENT MEASURES
              OF AUTHORITY FIGURES.

TYPE OF HOUSEHOLD

| | MALE | | | FEMALE | | |
VARIABLE	N	% PERSON CRIMES	N	% PERSON CRIMES	Tau b	Chi^2
Head of Household	219	19.3	119	16.2	.002	0.55
Main Decision Maker	110	23.6	236	19.1	.001	0.13
Main Wage Earner	202	22.3	129	17.1	.004	1.33
Most Influential Adult	90	14.4	266	22.6	.008	2.71

Significant values for Chi^2, df=1:

@ .001 level, 10.83
@ .01 level, 6.64
@ .02 level, 5.41
@ .05 level, 3.84

NOTE: The total N for each variable varies because of different
       numbers of unknowns, disagrees, etc.

TABLE 3.16. RELATIVE FREQUENCY OF DELINQUENTS HAVING A PERSON CRIME AS MOST SERIOUS OFFENSE ON THEIR J.A.D. RECORD BY TYPE OF HOUSEHOLD FOR DIFFERENT MEASURES OF AUTHORITY FIGURES FOR ALTERED FAMILIES ONLY (ABSENCE OF AT LEAST ONE PARENT).

TYPE OF HOUSEHOLD

	MALE		FEMALE			
VARIANCE	$\underline{N}$	% PERSON CRIMES	$\underline{N}$	% PERSON CRIMES	Tau b	Chi^2
Head of Household	35	34.3	120	18.3	.026	4.02
Main Wage Earner	34	38.2	109	17.4	.045	6.46
Main Decision Maker	18	44.4	136	22.8	.178	25.64

Significant values for Chi^2, df=1:

@ .001 level, 10.83
@ .01 level, 6.64
@ .02 level, 5.41
@ .05 level, 3.84

NOTE: The variable of "most influential adult" was not tested for altered families because of the small number of male households.

63

TABLE 3.17. RELATIVE FREQUENCY OF DELINQUENTS HAVING A
PERSON CRIME AS MOST SERIOUS OFFENSE ON
THEIR J.A.D. RECORD BY TYPE OF HOUSEHOLD
FOR DIFFERENT MEASURES OF AUTHORITY FIGURES
FOR INTACT FAMILIES ONLY.

TYPE OF HOUSEHOLD

	MALE			FEMALE		
VARIABLE	N	% PERSON CRIMES	N	% PERSON CRIMES	Tau b	Chi^2
Main Decision Maker	89	22.5	85	15.3	.008	1.46
Most Influential Adult	73	12.3	107	23.4	.019	3.45

Significant values for Chi^2, df=1"

@ .001 level, 10.83
@ .01 level, 6.64
@ .02 level, 5.41
@ .05 level, 3.81

NOTE: The variables of "head of household" and "main wage earner"
were not tested for intact families because, by definition,
there could be no female households in such cases.

These findings suggest that in families where the father is absent (the bulk of altered families consists of those without fathers), a "strong" female will act (at least slightly) as a check on violent behavior of young male delinquents. In other words, a dominant female in such situations is more successful in curbing the more overt masculine delinquent acts (assault, rape, etc.) only when the father is not present. Where a father is present, feminine influence will be insufficient as a counter balance to a father who may impart to the youth the somewhat more over masculine norms and values. At least the suggestion is that the father exerts sufficient influence to produce the non-significant results for intact families noted in Table 3.17. (This is true at least for the measure of main decision maker, the direction of the difference for most influential adult points to a support of the masculine protest hypothesis.)

In general however, the factor of matriarchy is of little importance for delinquency. If the results in this study are valid then a major rethinking of this issue is warranted. Perhaps the female-centered families in lower-class Negro settings are functional; they may represent an alternative family arrangement which is not, at the minimum, dysfunctional. It may well be that females in such situations are good teachers of "proper" masculine behavior thus avoiding any sexual ambiguity on the part of the young male. If this is true then more attention has to be directed to the study of the content of what is taught rather than who does the teaching. In a far more basic sense the findings may reflect an ignorance of what proper masculine and feminine behavior is within the Negro lower class. Perhaps we have imposed white middle-class standards and definitions of masculinity which have little relevance for lower-class Negroes, and in fact what we observe in such areas, raises no question to the subjects about sexual identification. In this context, perhaps we should limit Parsons'[51] remarks to the situation he was speculating about, middle-class families.

III. ORDINAL POSITION[52]

It might be argued that ordinal position would have importance for behavior because of possible differential experiences a youth may have. Adler in a psychoanalytic fashion argues that second-born children are treated as inferiors and consequently develop an inferiorty complex.[53] The youth turns to hostility and aggression in order to gain recognition and overcome the complex. Mannheim argues that this would be true for any youth who was not first-born (second, third, etc.).[54] Even if both men are correct, the type and direction of the aggression must be specified before this kind of explanation can be used for delinquency. Lees and Newson speculate that the oldest children become "individuals" because they learn to depend on themselves rather than a group of younger sibs, whereas intermediates are "group" influenced because of the influence of sibs already present.[55] The youngest are in a more "privileged" position (which counters Adler's argument) and at the same time free from responsibilities for brothers and sisters. They "learn to behave equally well - or badly - as members of a group and as individuals....[56]

The experience of the only child "....is liable to be (and to develop in them an attitude which is) a synthesis of that of eldests and youngests,"[57] in that they learn to be "individuals" and receive a large amount of maternal support. According to Lees and Newson the intermediates are more likely to commit offenses because they are more easily influenced by the "peer group" and the "gang". Once becoming delinquent, the intermediate tends to commit gang delinquencies, less serious crimes and is more easily reformed (again because he is easily influenced by a group). The oldest is less likely to become delinquent and when he does, commits the more serious crimes and is difficult to reform. The youngest are also less likely to become delinquent "...because tending to have privileged position in such homes and special place in relation to their mothers, they develop less inclination to be out and about..."[58]. Since the only child is a "synthesis" of the youngest and oldest, he will have about the same tendency toward delinquency as the youngest and oldest.

As far as is known, there are only three studies to date which employ control groups and which have investigated the relationship between ordinal position and delinquency. They are Sletto,[59], Gluecks,[60] and Nye.[61] One way of summarizing the results would be to rank order, ignoring the size of the differences, the ordinal groups in decreasing size of delinquency rates. The results of this summary, along with the findings of the present study, are given in Table 3.18.

TABLE 3.18.   RANK ORDER OF ORDINAL POSITION FOR
              DECREASING PROBABILITY OF DELINQUENCY,
              FOUR STUDIES.

Sletto (1934)[1]	Gluecks (1950)[2]	Nye (1958)[3]	Rosen (1967)[4]
Intermediate	Intermediate	Intermediate	Intermediate
Eldest	Eldest	Youngest	Only
Youngest	Youngest	Eldest	Youngest
	Only	Only	Eldest

[1]Raymond F. Sletto, "Sibling Position and Juvenile Delinquency", American Journal of Sociology, 39 (March, 1934), pp. 657-669. Study conducted in Minneapolis, 1928-1930. Delinquents were defined as "adjudicated delinquent" by the County Juvenile Court. The control group was selected from the public schools. Only children were excluded from the sample.

[2]Gluecks, op. cit. (see Table 3.1, note 5).

[3]Nye, op. cit. (see Table 3.1, note 6).

[4]For definition I (any J.A.D. record).

All four studies found the intermediates or "middle" males to have the highest probability of delinquency.[62] There is little agreement on the order of all the other groups of youths. The degrees of association for the same three studies were computed and are given in Table 3.19. (The independent variable is split into intermediates and all others.) All three studies show small associations (Tau b ranging from .002 to .015). The Glueck and Nye studies report significant findings at the .05 level.[63]

The findings for the North Philadelphia sample are basically in agreement (Table 3.20) with the results of the other studies.

TABLE 3.19. SUMMARY OF STUDIES CONCERNING ORDINAL
            POSITION (INTERMEDIATE VS. OTHERS) AND
            DELINQUENCY.

| RESEARCHER | DATE STUDY PUBLISHED | N | ASSOCIATION | |
			Tau b	Chi$^{2(1)}$
Sletto[2]	1934	1572	.002	3.13
Glueck and Glueck[3]	1950	1000	.015	14.97
Nye[4]	1958	1160	.005	6.28

[1]All Chi Square values are for one degree of freedom.
Significant values are: For .001 level, 10.83; for .01
level, 6.64; and for .05 level, 3.84.

[2]Sletto, op. cit. (see Table 3.18, note 1).

[3]Glueck and Glueck, op. cit. (see Table 3.1, note 5).

[4]Nye, op. cit. (see Table 3.1, note 6).

TABLE 3.20. DELINQUENCY STATUS (AS MEASURED BY THREE DEFINITIONS
OF DELINQUENCY) BY ORDINAL POSITION OF YOUTH.

DEFINITION OF DELINQUENCY[1]

ORDINAL POSITION	I		II		III	
		NON-		NON-		NON-
	J.D.	J.D.	J.D.	J.D.	J.D.	J.D.
Intermediate (N=380)						
n	165	215	103	277	130	250
%	43.4	56.6	27.1	72.9	34.2	65.8
Other (N=534)						
n	188	346	106	428	152	382
%	35.2	64.8	19.8	80.2	28.5	71.5
Total (N=914)						
n	353	561	209	705	282	632
%	38.6	61.4	22.8	77.2	29.8	70.2
Tau b	.007		.007		.004	
Chi^2	6.00		6.62		3.43	
Pr.Interval	.01 to .02		.01 to .02		.05 to .10	

[1]The three definitions are the same as given in Table 3.3.

Source: Appendix, Table 12.

The intermediate youths have the highest delinquency rate, with a small degree of association and significance (at the .05 level) for definitions I and II.[64]

Some interesting patterns emerge when the variable of ordinal position is partialed for family structure. Within intact families (Table 3.21), the intermediate child has the highest rate of delinquency. For definitions I and II this difference is significant. The situation is different, however, for the altered family (Table 3.22). The intermediate, youngest and only child groups all have fairly higher delinquency rates, while the oldest group is significantly lower from all others. The interesting finding is that the probability of the oldest child having a J.A.D. record is about the same in both types of family (31.9% for altered families and 32.2% for intact families), whereas all other sibling groups exhibited an increase in their delinquency rates (see Appendix, Table 13). Thus, the altered family seems to increase the likelihood of delinquency for all but the oldest male. Since the bulk of altered families involve an absent father, it is possible that the oldest male will be viewed by others, or view himself, as partly taking the place of the father. Consequently, the loss of the father may have a "maturating" effect on the oldest male which acts as a counter to the delinquency producing effect (to the extent that it exists) of an altered family.

TABLE 3.21.   DELINQUENCY STATUS (AS MEASURED BY THREE
DEFINITIONS) BY ORDINAL POSITION OF YOUTH
FOR INTACT FAMILIES (BOTH PARENTS PRESENT).

DEFINITION OF DELINQUENCY[1]

ORDINAL POSITIONS	I		II		III	
		NON-		NON-		NON-
Intermediate	J.D.	J.D.	J.D.	J.D.	J.D.	J.D.
(N=227)						
n	90	137	59	168	71	156
%	39.6	60.4	26.0	74.0	31.3	68.7
Others (N=292)						
n	90	202	44	248	71	221
%	30.8	69.2	15.1	84.9	24.3	75.7
Total (N=519)						
n	180	339	103	416	142	377
%	34.7	65.3	19.9	80.1	27.4	72.6
Tau b	.008		.018		.006	
Chi^2	4.39		9.58		3.11	
Pr. Interval	.02 to .05		.001 to .01		.05 to .10	

[1]The three definitions are the same as given in Table 3.3.

Source: Appendix, Table 13.

TABLE 3.22.   DELINQUENCY STATUS (AS MEASURED BY THREE DEFINITIONS OF DELINQUENCY) BY ORDINAL POSITION FOR ALTERED FAMILIES (AT LEAST ONE PARENT ABSENT).

DEFINITION OF DELINQUENCY[1]

ORDINAL POSITION	I		II		III	
	J.D.	NON-J.D.	J.D.	NON-J.D.	J.D.	NON-J.D.
Eldest (N=87)						
n	28	59	17	70	24	63
%	32.2	67.8	19.5	80.5	27.6	72.4
Others (N=253)						
n	124	129	78	175	102	151
%	49.0	51.0	30.8	69.2	40.3	59.7
Total (N=340)						
n	152	188	95	245	126	214
%	44.8	55.2	27.9	72.1	37.1	62.9
Tau_b	.022		.012		.013	
Chi^2	7.42		4.10		4.49	
Pr. Interval	.001 to .01		.02 to .05		.02 to .05	

[1]The three definitions are the same as given in Table 3.3.

Source: Appendix, Table 13.

IV. HOUSEHOLD SIZE

Bernard argues that large households are at a disadvantage compared to smaller households because material and psychological resources are dispersed over a larger number of persons.[65] Nye states that in small families:

> ...the resulting parent-child relation is more intimate
> and affectionate. Closer parent-child affectional ties
> should, in turn, result in more effective indirect con-
> trols and, perhaps, more effective internalization as
> well.[66]

The arguments of Bernard and Nye would lead one to expect a greater likelihood of delinquents coming from the larger households. However, this opinion is not necessarily held by all who have investigated the variable of family or household size. Bossard, for example, feels that the large family facilitates social control:

> Children in a large family discipline each other, ad-
> justments must be made to peers, not primarily to adults.
> Competitions between siblings are life-like, not 'pro-
> tected'. The disciplinary pressures are often more subtle
> than overt. The group is impatient with nonconforming
> members; there is ridicule for the odd one; there is dis-
> dain for the vexing transgressor.[67]

Thus, Bossard's argument would imply that the small family would have the greater probability of producing delinquency. (However, if the "norm" among the siblings was the violation of laws, the opposite may be true. Bossard speaks only about the mechanism of social control within the large family and not the direction it may take.)

The evidence to date finds that the large family or household has the greater tendency to produce delinquents. Mannheim, in his survey of the liter-ature, reports such a relationship.[68] Both the Gluecks[69] and Nye[70] find a greater tendency for the large households to contain delinquents, although the degree of association is fairly small.[71]

The findings from the North Philadelphia sample are very much the same (Table 3.23).[72] About 43% of those coming from seven persons and above house-holds had J.A.D. records, compared with 36% from households having six or fewer persons.[73] The difference was significant but small (Tau b = .005).

Would the effect of household size on delinquency be the same for an altered family as for an intact family? Bossard argues that in a small family the child receives more attention and "...grows up in a world that largely re-volves around him, and he thinks of himself accordingly."[74] If a child has the expectation of large amount of attention, a loss of parent or parents may prove to be a severe shock or trauma. (Although this may be somewhat modified in a lower-class Negro neighborhood where the relative instability of the father re-duces the likelihood of the youth receiving attention from the father.) Con-versely, Bossard contends that large families have more resistence to crisis:

...one of the things which easily strikes one about
large families is the tendency to take many crises,
especially minor ones, in stride. This is true much
more than in small families, perhaps for two main
reasons: One, the fact that crises occur so much more
frequently, and, second, that they are shared in by so
many more persons.[75]

If Bossard is correct, then delinquency would be more highly associated
with family structure in small households than in large households. The results
in Tables 3.24 and 3.25 tend to support Bossard. In large families there were
no significant differences between altered and intact families. However, there
were significant differences for the small households. In fact, this later
finding was the highest association reported in this study for any of the family
variables.

TABLE 3.23. DELINQUENCY STATUS (AS MEASURED BY THREE
             DEFINITIONS OF DELINQUENCY) BY HOUSEHOLD
             SIZE (NUMBER OF PERSONS).

DEFINITION OF DELINQUENCY[1]

HOUSEHOLD SIZE	I		II		III	
	J.D.	J.D.	J.D.	J.D.	J.D.	J.D.
Two to six (N=566)						
n	204	362	119	447	167	399
%	36.0	64.0	21.0	79.0	29.5	70.5
Seven to fifteen (N=355)						
n	153	202	93	262	118	237
%	43.1	56.9	26.2	73.8	33.2	66.8
Total (N=921)						
n	357	564	212	709	285	636
%	38.7	61.3	23.0	77.0	30.9	69.1
Tau b	.005		.004		.002	
Chi^2	4.57		3.29		1.42	
Pr. Interval	.02 to .05		.05 to .10		.20 to .30	

[1]The three definitions are the same as given in Table 3.3.

Source: Appendix, Table 14.

73

TABLE 3.24. DELINQUENCY STATUS (AS MEASURED BY THREE
DEFINITIONS OF DELINQUENCY) BY PRESENCE OR
ABSENCE OF PARENTS IN YOUTH'S FAMILY FOR
LARGE HOUSEHOLDS (7 TO 15 PERSONS).

DEFINITION OF DELINQUENCY[1]

TYPE OF FAMILY	I		II		III	
	J.D.	NON-J.D.	J.D.	NON-J.D.	J.D.	NON-J.D.
Altered[2] (N=99)						
n	49	50	30	69	39	60
%	49.5	50.5	30.3	69.7	39.4	60.6
Intact[3] (N=235)						
n	97	138	59	176	74	161
%	41.3	58.7	25.1	74.9	31.5	68.5
Total (N=334)						
n	146	188	89	245	113	221
%	43.8	56.2	26.8	73.2	33.9	66.1
Tau b	.006		.003		.006	
Chi^2	1.91		0.96		1.94	
Pr. Interval	.10 to .20		.30 to .50		.10 to .20	

[1]The three definitions are the same as given in Table 3.3.

[2]At least one parent absent.

[3]Both parents present.

Source: Appendix, Table 15.

74

TABLE 3.25. DELINQUENCY STATUS (AS MEASURED BY THREE DEFINITIONS OF DELINQUENCY) BY PRESENCE OR ABSENCE OF PARENTS IN YOUTH'S FAMILY FOR SMALL HOUSEHOLDS (2 TO 6 PERSONS).

DEFINITION OF DELINQUENCY[1]

TYPE OF FAMILY	I		II		III	
	J.D.	NON-J.D.	J.D.	NON-J.D.	J.D.	NON-J.D.
Altered[2] (N=245)						
n	106	139	67	178	89	156
%	43.3	56.7	27.3	72.6	36.3	63.7
Intact[3] (N=287)						
n	84	203	45	242	69	218
%	29.3	70.7	15.7	84.3	24.0	76.0
Total (N=532)						
n	190	342	112	420	158	374
%	35.7	64.3	21.1	78.9	29.7	70.3
Tau b	.050		.020		.018	
Chi^2	26.68		10.84		9.52	
Pr. Interval	<.001		<.001		.001 to .01	

[1]The three definitions are the same as given in Table 3.3.

[2]At least one parent absent.

[3]Both parents present.

Source: Appendix, Table 15.

V. CONCLUSION

Table 3.26 summarizes the results of the family variables investigated in this chapter. For the total sample (zero-order association) there were several variables significantly associated (at the .05 level) with delinquency. Of the eight variables included, six were significant for definition I, two for definition II, and four for definition III. However, all eight variables exhibited a small degree of association with no single variable accounting for more than 1.2% of the variance. Thus, any one of the eight variables by itself cannot be considered important enough to discriminate between the delinquent and non-delinquent in a high delinquent lower-class Negro area. And it is quite likely that some combination of the eight family variables will not improve the situation drastically. If all eight variables were independent of one another, and no interactions were operating, then all eight could not account for more than 6% of the variance.[76] In all likelihood this figure would be lower because for one it is fairly obvious that the variables are not orthogonal (e.g., sex of household head and sex of main wage earner), and, secondly, the partial association found no dramatic interaction.[77] To the extent that comparisons were possible with earlier studies for the same or similar variables, it seems that the findings, in this chapter, of small but significant associations are consistent with the earlier work.

The partial association analysis seems to add very little to our knowledge of the basic problem, with the possible exception of household size and altered family. The altered family proved to be moderately critical for small households in producing a greater probability of delinquency.

No major differences were found between the three definitions of delinquency. In general, definition I, the presence of any J.A.D. record, proved in most cases to have the highest association. However, the differences in the Tau b's were almost invariably less than .01. Consequently, it seems that little is gained by utilizing definitions predicated on seriousness of delinquency acts.

To conclude, the family variables which ecological research has suggested to be important, have failed to account for individual delinquency in a high delinquent area.

TABLE 3.26. SUMMARY TABLE FOR ASSOCIATION OF FAMILY VARIABLES AND DELINQUENCY STATUS (AS MEASURED BY THREE DEFINITIONS OF DELINQUENCY).

VARIABLE	N	DEFINITION OF DELINQUENCY[1]					
		I		II		III	
		Tau b	Chi^2	Tau b	Chi^2	Tau b	Chi^2
TOTAL SAMPLE							
Altered Family	866	.012	10.13[2]	.009	7.88[2]	.011	9.27[2]
Presence of Adult Males	849	.004	3.14	<.001	0.25	.003	2.63
Sex of Household Head	863	.009	7.85[2]	.003	2.76	.006	5.52[2]
Sex of Main Wage Earner	860	.011	9.33[2]	.004	3.65	.005	4.02[2]
Sex of Decision Maker	894	.010	8.85[2]	.002	1.43	.008	7.33[2]
Sex of Most Influential Adult	915	<.001	0.01	.002	2.13	<.001	0.14
Ordinal Position	914	.007	6.00[3]	.007	6.62[3]	.004	3.43
Household Size	921	.005	4.57[4]	.004	3.29	.002	1.42
INTACT FAMILIES							
Sex of Decision Maker	508	.002	0.94	<.001	0.06	<.001	0.02
Sex of Most Influential Adult	519	.004	2.15	.004	1.99	<.001	0.04
Ordinal Position	519	.008	4.39[4]	.018	9.58[2]	.006	3.11
ALTERED FAMILIES							
Status of Missing Parent	317	.002	0.60	<.001	0.03	<.001	0.03
Sex of Head	337	.008	2.82	.002	0.80	.001	0.03
Sex of Main Wage Earner	309	<.001	0.10	.009	2.74	.006	1.94
Sex of Decision Maker	336	.001	0.32	.004	1.27	<.001	0.01
Ordinal Position	340	.022	7.42[2]	.012	4.10[4]	.013	4.49[4]
SMALL HOUSEHOLDS							
Altered Family	532	.050	26.68[2]	.020	10.84[2]	.018	9.52[2]
LARGE HOUSEHOLDS							
Altered Family	334	.006	1.91	.003	0.96	.006	1.94

TABLE 3.26. SUMMARY TABLE FOR ASSOCIATION OF FAMILY
            VARIABLES AND DELINQUENCY STATUS (AS
            MEASURED BY THREE DEFINITIONS OF DELIN-
            QUENCY).
                        (Cont'd)

[1] The three definitions are the same as given in
Table 3.3.

[2] Significant @ .01 level.

[3] Significant @ .02 level.

[4] Significant @ .05 level.

Footnotes:

1. There is a tendency in this kind of analysis for the "evil causes evil" fallacy to enter. If an event A is "bad" or "evil", then all events associated with A are _ipso facto_ "bad" or "evil". See Gwynn Netler, "Good Men, Bad Men, and the Perception of Reality", Sociometry, 24 (September, 1961), pp. 279-294.

2. David J. Bordua, "Delinquency Theory and Research in the United States: Major Trends since 1930", <u>Kolner Zietschrift für Soziologie und Sozialpsychologie</u>, Sonderheft 2 (1957), states that the dominant emphasis for sociologists since the 1930's is on such concerns as delinquency values and social structure, thus relegating the family to a secondary role as a factor in delinquency. Psychologists, especially William Healy and Augusta F. Bronner, <u>New Light on Delinquency and Its Treatment</u>, New Haven: Yale University Press, 1936, are the behavioral scientists who have stressed the family, especially family interaction, as the major factor in delinquency.

3. A 1965 Gallup poll indicated that over half of the respondents' answers to the question "what they thought was responsible for the increase in crime" could be classified as family or "poor parental guidance". No other single response was nearly as frequent ("moral breakdown", "discrimination", "pornography", "television", etc.), with the next most frequent category being "moral standards breaking down" (6% of the responses). Cited in President's Commission on Law Enforcement and Administration of Justice, <u>The Challenge of Crime in a Free Society</u>, United States Government Printing Office: Washington, D.C., 1967, p. 50.
    Michael Gordon, (<u>Juvenile Delinquency in the American Novel, 1905-1965: A Study in the Sociology of Literature</u>, unpublished Doctoral Dissertation, University of Connecticut, 1967), in his survey of 19 popular periodicals (Life, The Nation, Saturday Evening Post, etc.) for the period 1905-1965 finds the family the one factor continuously cited as a cause of delinquency. In the most recent period (1953-1965) the psychodynamic factors within the family are stressed. There is also a greater frequency than in earlier periods to implicate factors external to the family (poverty, unemployment, etc.), but the family still has remained prominent.

4. Robert Bell, "The One-Parent Family: A Conceptual View", unpublished paper, 1965.

5. The principal reason for proposing the modification is that no data is available for this study to evaluate the functional adequacy of the parents who are present.

6. Donald R. Peterson and Wesley C. Becker, "Family Interaction and Delinquency" in Herbert C. Quay (Editor), Juvenile Delinquency, Princeton, New Jersey, D. Van Nostrand Company, 1965, p. 69. They reach this conclusion after a survey of several studies (several of which are included in Table 3.1 below) by noting the differences in the proportion of broken homes between delinquents and non-delinquents. This is a dubious procedure

for two reasons: (1) the data is percentaged in the wrong direction, it should be the percent difference between delinquents and non-delinquents within broken homes. (See Hans Zeisel, _Say It With Figures_, New York, Harper and Brothers, 1957); and (2) the strength of the relationship cannot be determined in this manner.

The authors do state that the broken home is not a "direct cause", but still claim, in terms of variance accounted for, that the variable is important.

7. Herman Mannheim, _Comparative Criminology_, Boston: Houghton-Mifflin Company, 1965, p. 618.

8. Richard R. Korn and Lloyd W. McCorkle, _Criminology and Penology_, New York Henry Holt and Company, 1959, p. 247.

9. This evaluation is a subjective one based on an unsystematic review of eight major textbooks in criminology.

10. Mannheim, _op. cit._, is an example of this type of criticism.

11. Studies which have questioned the general assertion that "broken home" is detrimental to children (on many dependent variables) are Lee G. Burchinal, "Characteristics of Adolescents from Unbroken, Broken, and Reconstituted Families", _Journal of Marriage and Family Living_, 26 (February, 1964), pp. 44-51; William Goode, _After Divorce_, Glencoe, Illinois: The Free Press, 1956, pp. 307-329; Paul H. Landis, _The Broken Home in Teenage Adjustments_, Washington Agricultural Experiment Stations Bulletin No. 542, June, 1953; F. Ivan Nye, "Child Adjustment in Broken and Unhappy Unbroken Homes", _Marriage and Family Living_, 19 (November, 1957), pp. 356-361.

Those who have questioned the specific assertion that "broken home" is the critical factor for delinquency and have argued instead the importance of "interaction" are: Sheldon Glueck and Eleanor Glueck, _Unraveling Juvenile Delinquency_, New York: Commonwealth Fund, 1950; F. Ivan Nye, (1957), _op. cit._; F. Ivan Nye, _Family Relationships and Delinquent Behavior_, New York: John Wiley and Sons, 1958; Hyman Rodman and Paul Grams, "Juvenile Delinquency and the Family: A Review and Discussion", unpublished paper, prepared for the President's Commission on Law Enforcement and Administration of Justice, 1967; Joan McCord and William McCord, "The Effects of Parental Role Model in Criminality" in Ruth Cavan (Editor) _Readings in Juvenile Delinquency_, Philadelphia: J.P. Lippincott, 1964, pp. 170-180.

12. Jackson Toby, "The Differential Impact of Family Disorganization", _American Sociological Review_, 22 (October, 1957), pp. 505-512.

13. See Hans Zeisel, _op. cit._

14. There is some evidence that family structure is a factor in the judicial decision to commit a youth to a correctional institution. Therefore, it is possible that the use of an institutional population would tend to inflate the proportion of "broken homes" among delinquents. See Richard S. Sterne, _Delinquent Conduct and Broken Homes_, New Haven College and University Press, 1964, pp. 45.

15. Leo A. Goodman and William H. Kruskal, "Measures of Association for Cross Classifications", <u>Journal of the American Statistical Association</u>, 49 (December, 1954), pp. 732-764.

16. Other "control" groups were used in his study (e.g., Negro, middle-class boys); however, for purposes of this paper, comparisons with lower-class youths were the only ones utilized.

17. The question asked of the youth was, "Whom did you live with when growing up?"

18. Gordon Barker, "Family Factors in the Ecology of Juvenile Delinquency", <u>Journal of Criminal Law and Criminology</u>, 30 (January-February, 1940), pp. 681-691.

19. Clifford Shaw and H. D. McKay, "Are Broken Homes a Causative Factor in Juvenile Delinquency?", <u>Social Forces</u>, 10 (May, 1932), p. 517.

20. H. A. Weeks and Margaret G. Smith, "Juvenile Delinquency and Broken Homes in Spokane, Washington", <u>Social Forces</u>, 18 (October, 1939), p. 51.

21. Maurice Connery, <u>An Ecological Study of Juvenile Delinquency</u>, unpublished Ph. D. dissertation, Columbia University, New York, 1960, p. 58.

22. The proportion of youths having a J.A.D. record (38.2%) is very similar to that of the total sample of 921 (38.7%).

23. Sterne, <u>op. cit</u>., p. 28. Raymond Illsley and Barbara Thompson, "Women from Broken Homes", <u>The Sociological Review</u>, 9 (March, 1961), pp. 27-54, is perhaps the best single study of broken homes, and it reports differences between women coming from homes broken by death and those broken by separation or divorce for such items as subsequent illegitimacy, leaving school at minimum age, marrying semi-skilled or unskilled workers and employment within manual jobs. Unfortunately, delinquency or criminality was not one of the variables considered.

24. Sterne, <u>op. cit</u>., p. 60. Serious offenses in his study were larceny, burglary, weapons, sex offenses, (other then fornication), aggravated assault and battery, and robbery. Minor offenses were juvenile status offenses, simple assault and battery, and fornication. In addition, Sterne found no significant association between "broken home" and the seriousness of delinquency.

25. This conclusion is tentative because of the absence of one single "ideal" study. Although only the studies in Table 3.1 which reported the highest association (namely the Gluecks and Browning) were chosen for more detailed criticising; the other studies have their faults as well. Therefore, it is quite possible that another alternative interpretation is possible; the studies which find low associations do so because of faulty methodology. If I were to design an ideal study to test the association between "broken home" and delinquency, it would have the following features: (1) a probability sample of youths, ages 7-17; (2) police or J.A.D. (in those cities which have similar agencies) contact rather than court hearings; (3) determine the nature of the break (death, desertion, etc.) and time

of break; and (4) what subsequent arrangements are made for the rearing of the youth.

26. Bell, op. cit.

27. Ibid., p. 6.

28. John Bowlby, Maternal Care and Mental Health, Geneva: World Health Organization, 1952.

29. Siri Ness, "Mother-Child Separation and Delinquency", British Journal of Delinquency, 10 (July, 1959), pp. 22-33.

30. Ibid., p. 26.

31. Robert G. Andry, "Faulty Paternal and Maternal-Child Relationships, Affection and Delinquency", British Journal of Delinquency, 8 (July, 1959) pp. 34-38).

32. See Appendix, Table 1.

33. This seems to be the "major conclusion" of the widely debated "Moynihan Report", United States Department of Labor, The Negro Family: The Case for National Action, Washington, D. C., United States Government Printing Office, 1965.

34. Thomas Pettigrew, A Profile of the Negro American, Princeton, New Jersey: D. Van Nostrand Company, 1964, pp. 15-24.

35. Walter B. Miller, "Lower Class Culture as a Generating Milieu of Gang Delinquency", Journal of Social Issues, 14, Number 3 (1958), pp. 5-19.

36. Talcott Parsons, "The Social Structure of the Family", in Ruth Wanda Anshen (Editor), The Family: Its Function and Destiny, Revised Edition, New York: Harper and Brothers, 1959, pp. 257-258.

37. The data on "broken home" can in a sense be used to test this proposition. This is so since most of the "broken homes" involve an absent father. However, as will be shown below it is possible to have a father present who is ineffectual or a "father substitute" if the father is absent, thus limiting the use of "broken home" as an index of matriarchy.

38. Ray A. Tennyson, "Family Structure and Delinquent Behavior", in Malcolm W. Klein (Editor), Juvenile Gangs in Context, Englewood Cliffs, New Jersey Prentice-Hall, 1967, pp. 57-69. It is not quite clear how the author measured dominance in the family.

39. See Appendix, Table 1.

40. In addition to 46 adult-youth disagreements over the presence of the father there were 25 disagreements involving other adult males. These latter disagreements were only for those families where there was agreement that the father was absent.

41. Jessie Bernard, <u>Marriage and Family among Negroes</u>, Englewood Cliffs, New Jersey: Prentice-Hall Inc., 1966, p. 126.

42. U.S. Bureau of Census, U.S. Census of Population; 1960: <u>General Population Characteristics, Pennsylvania Final Report</u> PC (1)-40B, U.S. Government Printing Office, Washington, D.C., 1961, p. x. The reason for attempting to construct a similar definition to that of the census was to allow for the possibility of some future comparisons with census derived data.

43. The interviewer was instructed to limit "family" in these two questions to only those living in the household at time of the interview.

44. Since only the youth's response was used to determine decision maker, most influential adult and main wage earner, there could be no youth-adult disagreements. No attempt was made to see if there was a youth-adult disagreement on the presence of the person who the youth designated on these three questions. Thus, to be precise, these variables are who the youth perceives to be in the position in question. The disagreements were omitted for household head to obtain some measure of who is present.

45. The agreement of the results on head, main wage earner and decision maker are to be expected because of the probably high inter-correlation of these three variables.

46. The fact that 54% of the intact families had females making most of the important family decisions (at least this is the way the youth saw it) is consistent with the findings of Rainwater. He reports that wives tend to make most of the decisions in the lower-class Negro families because the husbands are "unstable" and fail to take responsibility as fathers and husbands. ("Crucible of Identity: The Negro Lower-Class Family" in Talcott Parsons and Kenneth B. Clark (Editors), <u>The Negro American</u>, Boston: Houghton Mifflin Company, 1966, p. 178.)

47. Associations were not computed for head of household and main wage earner because, for the former, there would be no female heads of intact families by definition; for the latter, only 26 female main wage earners were reported for intact families.

48. In the case of altered families, the variable of most influential was not tested because of the small number (14) of "male households" for this measure.

49. Pettigrew, <u>op</u>. <u>cit</u>., p. 18-20, reports some findings that support this hypothesis.

50. See W. B. Miller, <u>op</u>. <u>cit</u>., and Talcott Parsons, <u>op</u>. <u>cit</u>.

51. Parsons, <u>op</u>. <u>cit</u>.

52. The term "ordinal position" is being used in preference to the term "birth order". The former refers to an ordering by age of siblings in a household and the latter to a sequential order of actual births of sibs. The two are not necessarily the same because it is possible for sibs to be separated (death, institutionalization, separate foster parents, living

with separate relatives), thus resulting in a different ordering of sibs than would be expected from birth order. Since the major premise underlying the present discussion is that youths have different experiences because of the presence or absence of other sibs, the ordinal position seems more appropriate. Consequently, the notion utilized in this study will be "ordinal position" within the household at the time of the study. No information is available on length of time the youth has been in a specified ordinal position or if there are sibs living elsewhere.

53. Cited in Mannheim, op. cit., p. 612.

54. Idem.

55. J. P. Lees and L. J. Newson, "Family or Sibship Position and Some Aspects of Juvenile Delinquency", British Journal of Delinquency, 5 (July, 1954), pp. 46-65.

56. Ibid., p. 62.

57. Idem.

58. Ibid., p. 63.

59. Raymond F. Sletto, "Sibling Position and Juvenile Delinquency", American Journal of Sociology, 39 (March, 1934), pp. 657-669.

60. Gluecks, op. cit.

61. Nye, op. cit.

62. Lees and Newson, op. cit., report that the intermediate group in a "working class" sample of English youths have the greatest proportion of delinquents. This conclusion is reached by finding a larger proportion of intermediate youths among their sample of delinquents than were found in the general population. No explicit control group was employed.

63. Barker, op. cit., is the only study to report ecological findings for ordinal position and delinquency. He concludes that ordinal position is not important. However, his analysis was the same as reported for "broken home" and therefore the same criticisms pertain.

64. The results on delinquency and ordinal position may be confounded with family size. If family size is associated with delinquency, then by necessity intermediacy would in general have higher delinquency rates (intermediates must come from families where at least three children are present. In order to test this, the sample was divided into large households (7-15 persons) and small households (2-6 persons). Intermediates for both groups had the highest delinquency rates (41.7% for small households and 44.5% for large households). Thus, on the basis of this, one test, household size, is not a confounding variable.

65. Bernard, op. cit., p. 131.

66. Nye, op. cit., p. 37.

67. James H. S. Bossard, Parent and Child, Philadelphia: University of Pennsylvania Press, 1953, p. 61.

68. Mannheim, op. cit., p. 610.

69. Gluecks, op. cit., p. 89.

70. Nye, op. cit., p. 37.

71. For the Gluecks, about 46% of the youths from households below 7 were delinquent, and 52% of the large households (8 and above) were delinquent. The Tau b was .005. In the Nye study, 28% of youths from the one and two person families were the "more delinquent", and 35% of the youths from three person and above families were classified as "more delinquent". The Tau b for the Nye research was .007.

72. Household size was obtained from the responses of the youth since he was the only one asked to list all the members in the household.

73. The particular dividing point between small and large households was chosen because it maximized the association between delinquency (definition I) and household size. For the rationale for such a procedure see Robert A. Gordon, "Issues in the Ecological Study of Delinquency", American Sociological Review, 32 (December, 1967), p. 940.

74. Bossard, op. cit., p. 91.

75. Ibid., p. 107.

76. This is the result of the simple addition of Tau b's for all 8 variables for definition I. This is not quite a legitimate procedure because of the varying sample size of each variable.

77. The one possible exception is the combination of household size and presence of parents which produced a small amount of interaction. The Tau b for both of these variables combined was .021.

CHAPTER FOUR

SOCIO-ECONOMIC VARIABLES

Socio-economic variables are of classic and continuing interest in the study of delinquency, and the research, theory and speculation in this area are voluminous. Although there is a fair amount of debate on the nature and direction of the relationship, the bulk of the evidence for official statistics indicates that the lower class has a higher probability of producing delinquent However, little is still known concerning the importance of socio-economic vari ables in a high delinquency area. The variables to be investigated in this study as indicators of socio-economic position of the youth are: (1) occupational status of the main wage earner; (2) educational attainment of the main wage earner; (3) tenure status of the dwelling unit (owner-occupied or not owner-occupied); and (4) room density (persons/room). As shown in Chapter Two, the study area is low with respect to occupational prestige, educational level and home ownership and high in room density.

I. OCCUPATIONAL STATUS

The ecological evidence indicates that areas having a higher proportion of blue collar, especially unskilled, workers have a greater probability of having higher delinquency rates. For example, Connery reports a product-moment r of -0.93 between delinquency rates and an occupational scale constructed on the basis of the Edwards classification schema.[2] Chilton, utilizing the proportion of persons 14 and above employed as service workers or laborers as a measure of occupational status, found a correlation of 0.68 in 1950 and 0.61 in 1960 between delinquency rates and occupation.[3]

The studies of individual delinquency and occupational status present a different picture. Hardt and Peterson's study[4] of 180 boys in a "predominantly Negro" high delinquent neighborhood found 40% of the blue collar boys and 25% of the white collar boys to have a police record. However, the difference was non-significant.[5] The finding of non-significance was also true for a low de linquent, middle income area. Reiss and Rhodes[6] report a higher delinquency rate for the blue collar group (8.8%) than for the white collar group (6.2%); however, the variance accounted for is only 0.6%.[7] Within the low status area[8] there was practically no relationship between occupation and delinquency (Tau b = .004), while at the same time the delinquency rate in the low status area for each occupational group was approximately doubled its overall rate. Thus, the status of the area is more important than the occupation of the youth's father (or head of household). Within high and delinquent areas there was also no relationship (Tau b less than .001) between occupational status and indivi- dual delinquency. Importance of the area is also demonstrated by the research of Clark and Wenninger.[9] Two neighborhoods in Chicago were demarcated: "Lower urban", which was a predominantly lower class[10] Negro area, and an "upper urban" which was a very "wealthy" suburb of Chicago. Youths from the "lower urban" area reported a significantly larger number of "illegal acts". At the same time no class differences were found within the two areas. The general conclusion suggested by these three studies is that the occupational status of the area

86

is a more important variable than the occupational class of the youth.

Significant differences between occupational groups for this sample are found for all three definitions (Table 4.1). For example, approximately 33% of the boys had J.A.D. record who came from households where the main wage earner was skilled or white collar worker, compared with 42.1% for the un- skilled and housewife group. The strength of the association was small for all three definitions (Tau b was .008 for definitions I and III and .013 for de- finition II).

TABLE 4.1. DELINQUENCY STATUS (AS MEASURED BY THREE DEFINITIONS OF DELINQUENCY) BY OCCUPATION OF MAIN WAGE EARNER IN YOUTH'S HOUSEHOLD.

DEFINITION OF DELINQUENCY

OCCUPATION	I^1		II^2		III^3	
	J.D.	NON- J.D.	J.D.	NON- J.D.	J.D.	NON- J.D.
Skilled and White Collar (N=333)						
n	110	223	56	277	85	248
%	33.1	66.9	16.8	83.2	25.6	74.4
Housewives and Un- skilled (N=541)						
n	228	313	144	397	185	356
%	42.1	57.9	26.7	73.3	34.2	65.8
Total (N=874)*						
n	338	536	200	674	270	604
%	38.7	61.3	22.9	77.1	30.9	69.1
Tau b	.008		.013		.008	
Chi^2	7.21		11.21		7.25	
Pr. Interval	.001 to .01		<.001		.001 to .01	

[1] J.A.D. record, any offense

[2] Offense against property or person as most serious offense on J.A.D. record.

[3] J.A.D. record, excluding juvenile status offense as most serious offense.

*Excludes 47 unknowns.

Source: Appendix, Table 16.

II. EDUCATION

The seven ecological studies listed in Table 4.2 show a moderate associa-tion between delinquency rates and educational level of the area. The Gluecks' study is the only one that has investigated the educational status of the youth's household.[11] Rearranging their data into two categories of parents' education ((1) both had none or "one or both parents attended or completed grade school, and (2) one or both parents attended or completed high school or vocational school,") yields a Tau b of .005 and chi square of 4.62 (significant at the .05 level).

In the present study the educational level of the main wage earner was di-vided into a low (0-9 years) and high (10-16 years) group.[12] The youths coming from low education households had a greater probability (44.3%) of having a J.A.D. record than the high education group (34.0%) (see Table 4.3). This dif-ference was small (Tau b = .011) although significant. In addition, there was a significant difference in the same direction for definition III. (Tau b = .008).

TABLE 4.2. PRODUCT MOMENT ZERO ORDER CORRELATIONS BETWEEN DELINQUENCY RATES AND MEDIAN YEARS OF SCHOOL COMPLETED BY PERSONS 25 YEARS AND OLDER FOR SEVEN ECOLOGICAL STUDIES.

INVESTIGATION	PLACE	DATE	r
Lander[1]	Baltimore	1939-42	-.51
Bordua[2]	Detroit	1948-50	-.47
Chilton[3]	Indianapolis	1948-50	-.68
Bates[4]	St. Louis	1957	-.19
Chilton[5]	Indianapolis	1958-60	-.56
Conlin[6]	Baltimore	1958	-.13
Connery[7]	St. Paul	1958-60	-.54

[1]Bernard Lander, Towards An Understanding of Juvenile Delinquency, New York: Columbia University Press, 1954, p. 36.

[2]Donald J. Bordua, "Juvenile Delinquency and Anomie", Social Pro-blems, 6 (Winter, 1958), p. 230-238. (The product moment r were not given in this paper, but was cited in Chilton, see note 3.)

[3]Ronald J. Chilton, Social Factors and the Residential Distribution of Official Delinquents, Indianapolis, Indiana, unpublished Ph.D. Disser-tation, Indiana University, 1962, p. 67.

[4]William M. Bates, The Ecology of Juvenile Delinquency in St. Louis, unpublished Ph.D. Dissertation, Washington University, St. Louis, Mo., 1959, p. 97.

TABLE 4.2. PRODUCT MOMENT ZERO ORDER CORRELATIONS BETWEEN
           DELINQUENCY RATES AND MEDIAN YEARS OF SCHOOL
           COMPLETED BY PERSONS 25 YEARS AND OLDER FOR
           SEVEN ECOLOGICAL STUDIES. (CONT'D)

[5]Chilton, op. cit., p. 67.

[6]James J. Conlin, An Area Study of Juvenile Delinquency in Baltimore, Maryland, unpublished Ph.D. Dissertation, St. Louis University,
St. Louis, Mo. 1961, p. 28.

[7]Maurice F. Connery, An Ecological Study of Juvenile Delinquency
in St. Paul, unpublished Ph.D. Dissertation, Columbia University, New
York, 1960, p. 56.

TABLE 4.3. DELINQUENCY STATUS (AS MEASURED BY THREE DEFINITIONS
           OF DELINQUENCY) BY YEARS OF EDUCATION COMPLETED FOR
           MAIN WAGE EARNER IN YOUTH'S HOUSEHOLD.

DEFINITION OF DELINQUENCY[1]

YEARS OF EDUCATION	I		II		III	
	J.D.	NON-J.D.	J.D.	NON-J.D.	J.D.	NON-J.D.
Low, 0-9 years (N=418)						
n	185	233	108	310	148	270
%	44.3	55.7	25.8	74.2	35.4	64.6
High, 10-16 years (N=435)						
n	148	287	88	347	118	317
%	34.0	66.0	20.2	79.8	27.1	72.9
Total (N=853)*						
n	333	520	196	657	266	587
%	39.1	60.9	23.0	77.0	31.2	68.8
Tau b	.011		.004		.008	
Chi^2	9.38		3.70		6.66	
Pr. Interval	.001 to .01		.05 to .10		.001 to .01	

[1]The three definitions are the same as given in
Table 4.1.

*Excludes 68 unknowns.

Source: Appendix, Table 17.

III. OWNER-OCCUPANCY

Home ownership is a widely used indicator of socio-economic level and commitment to community. First of all, it is fairly obvious that higher income groups have greater financial resources to own their own homes than low income groups, and in fact there is a positive relationship between income and home ownership.[13] Besides the obvious relationship with income, there have bee several authors who have argued that home ownership reflects stability. For ex ample, Lillian Cohen states:

> A comparison of the social characteristics of owner and tenant
> families in the twenty-two largest metropolitan districts with
> a population of 500,000 or over, April, 1940, reveals that home-
> owner families are more inclined than are tenant families to have
> those characteristics which are generally regarded as 'stable'.
> Homeowner heads of families are, in general, older, have a higher
> income, move about less, and are often part of a 'normal family'.[14]

Lander contends that home ownership is an indicator of community stability and lack of "anomie".[15] Finally, Raab and Selznick are most enthusiastic in their support of the variable:

> Home ownership usually requires a measure of responsibility and
> sense of family unity. It implies permanence, steady employment,
> disciplined work habits, the existence of aspirations, the capa-
> city to plan for the future. Among the relatively impoverished
> members of the community, home ownership is probably one of the
> best indicators we have of social stability and family unity, co-
> hesiveness, and discipline.

> ....home ownership tends to select out families already fairly
> well integrated into society. It also gives individuals an addi-
> tional stake in community life. Together with home ownership is
> often....the chance to make friends, and efforts to achieve re-
> spectability and social acceptance. In home ownership areas,
> standards of conduct are apt to be higher than in rental areas.
> Children are likely to be more closely scrutinized and supervised
> by both parents and neighbors. Community approval and disapproval
> are probably readier and quicker to make themselves felt, and
> children are unlikely to live in an atmosphere of indifference.[16]

If the above speculation is correct, for both income and stability, one would expect a negative relationship between home ownership and delinquency.

The ecological studies have basically confirmed that such a relationship exists (see Table 4.4), by indicating that the probability is fairly good that areas of low owner-occupancy rates are high in delinquency. Surprisingly, ther have been almost no studies of individual delinquency and owner occupancy, witl the one exception of Weeks. In his research he obtained a contingency coeffi-cient of 0.462 (significant at the .05 level) between home ownership and delin-quency.[17] The study involved a city-wide population of youths and was not con-cerned with youths from high delinquent areas.

TABLE 4.4. PRODUCT-MOMENT ZERO-ORDER CORRELATIONS FOR
DELINQUENCY RATES AND RATES OF OWNER-OCCU-
PANCY FOR EIGHT ECOLOGICAL STUDIES.

INVESTIGATOR[1]	PLACE	DATE	r
Lander	Baltimore	1939-42	-0.80
Harlan and Wherry[2]	Birmingham	1940	-0.75
Bordua	Detroit	1948-50	-0.61
Chilton	Indianapolis	1948-50	-0.54
Bates	St. Louis	1957	-0.43
Chilton	Indianapolis	1958-60	-0.76
Conlin	Baltimore	1958	-0.25
Connery	St. Paul	1958-60	-0.74

[1]The sources of the individual studies in this table are the same as Table 4.2 with the exception of Harlan and Wherry.

[2]Howard Harlan and Jack Wherry, "Delinquency and Housing", Social Forces, 27 (October, 1948), p. 85.

The variable investigated in this study was owner-occupancy; in other words, did the youth come from a dwelling unit in which the owner lived (any relationship to the youth). Information on ownership was gathered subsequent to the time of the original interview and was the only data, outside of delinquency status, which was not supplied by the respondents.

The principal source for obtaining the name of the owner for each dwelling unit was the 1965-66 edition of the Philadelphia Real Estate Directory.[18] The directory lists, among other things, for every property in the city the name of owner, type of structure by use, type of construction, assessed value of both land and land cover, and date of last sale. In addition, the address of an absentee owner is listed. However, it became evident early in the research that not all absentee owners were listed as such. This was evidenced in several ways: (1) a few corporation names had no address listed; (2) some owners of a large number of properties in the area, who were known to live elsewhere, had no addresses given; and (3) a check of the Philadelphia Telephone Directory uncovered a few owners to be living elsewhere. In contrast to the above, there was a greater degree of certainty that owners who were listed at an alternative address are, in fact, absentee owners. This was confirmed by a check of the telephone directory. In not a single case (when the owner was listed in the telephone directory) was an absentee owner found to be living at the address of the property in question.

In those cases where the property was sold after the date of the adult interview, or where no listing was given in the Real Estate Directory (because of public housing, condemnation, recombining of parcels, demolition, etc.), th deed of the property was consulted in the Department of Records, Philadelphia City Government. By following this procedure only five of the 927 properties checked, could the name of the owner not be found. (These cases were eliminat from the final sample.) As an additional check on the Real Estate Directory all the names of the owners were checked in the 1964 telephone directory. Thi cannot be considered to be either a reliability or validity check since a fair proportion of the adult respondents were, for one reason or another, not liste in the telephone directory. However by following this procedure a few discrep ancies were uncovered. There is no way of knowing what proportion of those no listed in the telephone directory would have also shown discrepancies.

The dwelling unit was considered to be owner-occupied if one of the fol-lowing conditions was met:

(1) the full name of the owner and full name of adult respondent were the same;[19]
(2) the adult respondent was listed in the deed as part owner[20] if the surname of the owner and respondent differed;
(3) if the name of the owner and adult respondent were different, and the respondent was not listed as owner in the deed, then all of the following conditions had to be met: (a) the Real Estate Directory did not list the owner at a different address; (b) the owner's name is listed in the telephone directory at the same address as the adult respondent; (c) the phone number of the owner corresponds with the phone number given in either the adult or youth's questionnaire; (d) at least one adult old enough to be an owner (i.e., 21 or above) was listed by both youth and juvenile as living in the household.

Non-owner occupied dwelling units were those units which did not meet any of the above conditions for owner-occupied units.

There were 30 cases which did not meet conditions 1 or 2 for owner-occu-pancy, and the owner and/or adult respondent were not listed in the telephone directory. Because of this inability to use the telephone directory, there was less certainty in these cases that they were in fact not owner-occupied. However, since there is a greater likelihood that they are non owner-occupied, they were classified as such.

Approximately thirty percent of the youths in the sample came from owner-occupied units. This figure compares favorably with the 34.5% owner-occupied rate for non-white in the area in 1960.[21] Of the 281 youths of owner-occupied units, 77.9% came from units owned by one or both parents, 15.6% owned by anoth relative, and in 6.4% of the cases the relationship was not determined.

As can be seen from Table 4.5, only one definition (I) exhibited a signi-ficant difference with about 34% of the youths defined as delinquents coming from owner-occupied units and approximately 41% of the youths classified as de linquents coming from non-owner-occupied units.

TABLE 4.5. DELINQUENCY STATUS (AS MEASURED BY THREE
DEFINITIONS OF DELINQUENCY) BY OCCUPANCY
STATUS OF DWELLING UNIT OF YOUTH'S HOUSE-
HOLD.

DEFINITION OF DELINQUENCY[1]

OCCUPANCY STATUS	I		II		III	
	J.D.	NON-J.D.	J.D.	NON-J.D.	J.D.	NON-J.D.
Owner-occupied (N=281)						
n	94	187	57	224	79	202
%	33.5	66.5	20.3	79.7	28.1	71.9
Not Owner-Occupied (N=637)						
n	263	374	157	480	206	431
%	41.3	58.7	24.6	75.4	32.3	67.7
Total (N=918)*						
n	357	561	214	704	285	633
%	38.9	61.1	23.3	76.7	31.0	69.0

Tau b	.005	.002	.002
Chi^2	5.03	2.07	1.62
Pr. Interval	.02 to .05	.10 to .20	.20 to .30

[1]The three definitions are the same as given in Table 4.1.

*Excludes 3 unknowns.

Source: Appendix, Table 18.

93

The variable of home-ownership, however, accounted for less than 1% of the variability. Consequently, owner-occupancy cannot be considered to be an efficient discriminator.

Even though owner-occupancy is not important in general, it exhibits importance for female-based households (measured by sex of main wage earner) (see Table 4.6); the Tau b for Definition I is .014 (significant at the .05 level).

TABLE 4.6. DELINQUENCY STATUS (AS MEASURED BY THREE DEFINITIONS OF DELINQUENCY) BY OCCUPANCY STATUS OF DWELLING UNIT OF YOUTH'S HOUSEHOLD FOR FEMALE MAIN WAGE EARNER HOUSEHOLDS.

DEFINITIONS OF DELINQUENCY[1]

OCCUPANCY STATUS	I		II		III	
	J.D.	NON-J.D.	J.D.	NON-J.D.	J.D.	NON-J.D.
Owner-occupied (N=39)						
n	11	28	5	34	9	30
%	28.2	71.8	12.8	87.2	23.0	77.0
Not owner-occupied (N=274)						
n	126	148	76	198	101	173
%	46.0	54.0	27.7	72.3	36.8	63.2
Total (N=313)						
n	137	176	81	232	110	203
%	42.5	57.5	25.9	74.1	35.2	64.8
Tau b	.014		.013		.009	
Chi^2	4.38		3.96		2.84	
Pr. Interval	.02 to .05		.02 to .05		.05 to .10	

[1]The three definitions are the same as given in Table 4.1.

Source: Appendix, Table 19.

At the same time there is almost a complete absence of a relationship within male households (see Table 4.7).

TABLE 4.7. DELINQUENCY STATUS (AS MEASURED BY THREE DEFINITIONS OF DELINQUENCY) BY OCCUPANCY STATUS OF DWELLING UNIT OF YOUTH'S HOUSEHOLD FOR MALE MAIN WAGE EARNER HOUSEHOLDS.

DEFINITION OF DELINQUENCY[1]

OCCUPANCY STATUS	I		II		III	
	J.D.	NON-J.D.	J.D.	NON-J.D.	J.D.	NON-J.D.
Owner-occupied (N=214)						
n	71	143	44	170	62	152
%	33.2	66.8	20.6	79.4	29.0	71.0
Not owner-occupied (N=308)						
n	111	197	66	242	86	222
%	36.1	63.9	21.4	78.6	27.9	72.1
Total (N=522)						
n	182	340	110	412	148	374
%	34.8	65.2	21.1	78.9	28.4	71.6

Tau b	.001	$<.001$	$<.001$	
Chi^2	0.45	.05	$<.001$	
Pr. Interval	.50 to .70	.70 to .90	$>.90$	

[1]The three definitions are the same as given in Table 4.1.

Source: Appendix, Table 19.

Therefore, the significant overall association between owner-occupancy and delinquency is attributable only to the effect of ownership within the female household (i.e., there is statistical interaction between ownership and sex of main wage earner). The relationship for female households should be viewed with caution because of the disproportionately small number of female households coming from owner-occupied units.

IV. ROOM DENSITY

Room density may be considered to reflect three factors possibly related t delinquency: Socio-economic (X_1), privacy (X_2), and tension (X_3). There are several possible causal links with delinquency. If socio-economic position is associated with delinquency and overcrowding, then (if Y equals delinquency)

$$X_1 \longrightarrow Y$$

would follow. The lack of privacy and "living space" may increase the likeli-hood of the youth's spending a larger proportion of his waking hours outside the dwelling unit.[22] This may decrease the effectiveness of parental (or adult) control and/or increase the probability of interaction with delinquent peers. Thus,

$$X_2 \longrightarrow Y.$$

Overcrowding basically means as well, a greater likelihood of contact with hous hold members, which may increase the absolute number of strain-producing contac Or, as Burt has expressed it:

> Often far more serious in its ultimate effects, are the ceaseless
> friction and recurrent irritation, which, even among families the
> most patient and forbearing, can hardly be prevented, while a number
> of individuals, differing widely in wants and in pursuits according
> to their age and station, are kept jostling every day and all day
> long, in the closest personal proximity, within the four narrow walls
> of an overpacked apartment.[23]

James Plant, as well, argues that crowding produces, among other negative consequences, increased irritability for all concerned.[24] If irritability is associated with delinquency then another possible causal chain is:

$$X_3 \longrightarrow Y$$

There are of course, many possible combinations of the three independent vari-ables. The socio-economic factor may cause a decrease in privacy, or an increa in tension, which in turn may produce delinquency. Another possibility is that any two of the independent variables may simultaneously both be direct causes o delinquency. For example:

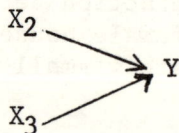

$$X_2 \searrow \atop X_3 \nearrow Y$$

In addition all three independent variables may be direct causes in the same sense as the above example. These are just a few of the possible causal system However, since there are no direct and independent measures of these three fact it is impossible to evaluate each of the many possible causal chains.

Ecological studies of delinquency represent the major portion of empirical knowledge on overcrowding and delinquency. These studies for the most part hav reported moderate correlations between overcrowding and delinquency (see Table 4.8).[25]

TABLE 4.8. PRODUCT-MOMENT ZERO-ORDER CORRELATIONS FOR DELIN-
            QUENCY RATES AND RATES OF OVERCROWDING FOR SEVEN
            ECOLOGICAL STUDIES.

INVESTIGATOR[1]	PLACE	DATE	r
Lander	Baltimore	1939-42	0.73
Bordua	Detroit	1948-50	0.65
Chilton	Indianapolis	1948-50	0.84
Bates	St. Louis	1957	0.31
Chilton	Indianapolis	1958-60	0.57
Conlin	Baltimore	1958	0.18
Connery	St. Paul	1958-60	0.76

[1]The sources of the individual studies in this table are
the same as Table 4.2.

Burt's study of a British population found an ecological correlation of 0.77 for
overcrowding (defined as more than two adults in one room, with two children
under ten equivalent to one adult), but a much lower correlation for individuals
(0.21), upon which he concludes:

> ......although juvenile delinquents usually come from
> overcrowded neighborhoods, they do not necessarily come
> from overcrowded homes.[26]

Loring, in his research on "disorganized" families, finds overcrowding to
be of some importance.[27] In his study a disorganized family was defined as
one known to the court and social work agencies (1942-1950) and having at least
one of the following "problems": Divorce, separation, juvenile delinquency,
parent-child problems, marital difficulties, sibling difficulties, non-support,
neglect of child, alcoholism, sex maladjustment, generational conflict, personality problems. Randomly selected non-problem families were matched with the
experimental group for family size, age and sex distribution, relationships
within the home, nationality, occupation of head, and rent. A total of 83 pairs
were finally utilized in the analysis. The seven significant factors found
were, in one manner or another, reflective of density (e.g., number of rooms,
space), but factors reflecting quality of housing (e.g., presence of bath, de-
terioration) were not significant.

In the present study, room density was simply computed by dividing total
household size by the number of rooms in the dwelling unit.[28] This particular
definition of density might, in a sense, be considered inadequate. It could
be argued that total living space, measured in square feet, is the important
dimension, and since rooms vary in size, the number of rooms is a poor indicator

of "living space". On the other hand private space, space which is divided an[d] separated from other space, may be in fact the crucial issue for privacy and tension. Compare the following two situations: (1) two people in a 20 by 20 foot room (density of 2 persons per room or 0.5 person per 100 square feet); and (2) two people in two separate 10 by 10 foot rooms (density of 1 person pe[r] room or 1 person per 100 square feet). Quite obviously in the latter situatio[n] there is less chance for contact, even though it can in one sense, person per 100 square feet, be considered to be more overcrowded than the former situatio[n]. Therefore, it is quite possible that walls and rooms may be more important tha[n] total square footage.[29]

Rather than use the term "overcrowded" in this study, the sample was divided into a low density group (0.20 - 0.80 persons per room) and a high densi[ty] group (0.82 - 4.00 persons per room).[30] As can be seen from Table 4.9, there [is] no significantly greater tendency for high density households to have delinque[nts] than low density households.

TABLE 4.9. DELINQUENCY STATUS (AS MEASURED BY THREE DEFINITIONS OF DELINQUENCY) BY ROOM DENSITY (PERSONS PER ROOM) IN YOUTHS'S HOUSEHOLD.

DEFINITION OF DELINQUENCY[1]

ROOM DENSITY	I		II		III	
	J.D.	NON-J.D.	J.D.	NON-J.D.	J.D.	NON-J.D.
Low, 0.20 - 0.80 (N=313)						
n	111	202	62	251	91	222
%	35.5	64.5	19.8	80.2	29.1	70.9
High, 0.82 - 4.00 (N=608)						
n	246	362	150	458	194	414
%	40.5	59.5	24.7	75.3	31.9	68.1
Total (N=921)						
n	357	564	212	709	285	636
%	38.7	61.3	23.0	77.0	30.9	69.1
Tau b	.002		.003		.001	
Chi^2	2.17		2.85		0.55	
Pr. Interval	.10 to .20		.05 to .10		.30 to .50	

[1]The three definitions are the same as given in Table 4.1.

Source: Appendix, Table 20.

V. "LOWER CLASS" vs. "WORKING CLASS"

In recent years there has been a growing awareness that the lower socio-economic class (as measured by income and occupation) is far from a homogeneous group. For example, Gans speaks about the lower socio-economic class as being composed of a "working class" and a "lower class" with each class representing two fairly divergent life styles or subcultures.[31] The "working class" is characterized as stable, "routine-seeking", and places great importance on the family. In contrast, the "lower-class" is "distinguished by the female-based family and the marginal male", and the emphasis is on "action". If such a distinction does in fact exist, then one would expect a greater likelihood of delinquents coming from "lower class" households.

In an attempt to evaluate the impact of this finer division of social class, in a lower socio-economic area, a crude and arbitrary index was constructed on the basis of three variables believed to measure the important dimensions. The three variables are: Sex of main wage earner (a measure of "female-based" household); occupation of main wage earner;[32] and owner-occupancy (a measure of stability). The eight groups, along with their delinquency rates (J.A.D. record), are given in Table 4.10. The two extreme groups are assumed to represent opposite poles of the social class continuum, with the others occupying some intermediate position.

As can easily be seen, the only major break in the continuum occurs with the last group, female, unskilled and non-owner-occupied. If this group is considered to be "lower class" and all others "working class", then a small but significant difference is noted (see Table 4.11.). However, this classification has not drastically increased the variability accounted for over the zero-order association of sex of main wage earner (see Table 3.7, Chapter Three). In the latter case 1.1 percent of the variability was explained, compared with 1.6 percent in the former.[33] Consequently, the variable of "lower class", to the extent to which it was validly measured, is not a major factor for delinquency in this Negro lower socio-economic area.

99

TABLE 4.10. DELINQUENCY STATUS (AS MEASURED BY PRESENCE OF J.A.D. RECORD) BY SEX AND OCCUPATION OF MAIN WAGE EARNER AND TENURE OF DWELLING UNIT[1] OF YOUTH'S HOUSEHOLD.

	J.A.D.		NON-J.A.D.		TOTAL	
	N	%	N	%	N	%
Male, skill., own.	35	30.2	81	69.8	116	100.0
Male, skill., non-own.	43	32.6	89	67.4	132	100.0
Female, skill., own.	6	31.6	13	68.4	19	100.0
Female, skill., non-own.	18	36.0	32	64.0	50	100.0
Male unskill., own.	36	36.7	62	63.3	98	100.0
Male unskill., non-own.	68	38.6	108	61.4	176	100.0
Female unskill., own.	5	25.0	15	75.0	20	100.0
Female unskill., non-own.	108	48.2	116	51.8	224	100.0
Unknown[2]	38	44.3	48	55.7	86	100.0
TOTAL	357	38.7	564	61.2	921	100.0

[1]For type of offense breakdown, see Appendix, Table 19.
[2]This includes every youth for which at least one of the three variables is unknown.

TABLE 4.11. DELINQUENCY STATUS (AS MEASURED BY THREE DEFINITIONS OF DELINQUENCY) BY SEX AND OCCUPATION OF MAIN WAGE EARNER AND OCCUPANCY STATUS OF DWELLING UNIT OF YOUTH'S HOUSEHOLD.

DEFINITION OF DELINQUENCY[1]

		I		II		III	
		J.D.	NON-J.D.	J.D.	NON-J.D.	J.D.	NON-J.D.
Female, unskilled and non-owner-occupied[2] (N=224)							
	n	108	116	65	159	87	137
	%	48.2	51.8	29.0	71.0	38.8	61.2
Others[3] (N=611)							
	n	211	400	126	485	171	440
	%	34.5	65.5	20.6	79.4	28.0	72.0
Total (N=835)							
	n	319	516	191	644	258	577
	%	38.2	61.8	22.9	77.1	30.9	69.1
Tau b		.016		.008		.001	
Chi[2]		12.99		6.55		9.04	
Pr. Interval		<.001		.01 to .02		.001 to .01	

[1]The three definitions are the same as given in Table 4.1.

TABLE 4.11.   DELINQUENCY STATUS (AS MEASURED BY THREE DEFINITIONS
              OF DELINQUENCY) BY SEX AND OCCUPATION OF MAIN WAGE
              EARNER AND OCCUPANCY STATUS OF DWELLING UNIT OF
              YOUTHS HOUSEHOLD (CONT'D).

[2]An indicator of "lower" class households.

[3]An indicator of "working" class households.

*Excludes 86 unknowns.

Source: Appendix, Table 19.

VI. CONCLUSION

The findings for the socio-economic variables are summarized in Table
4.12. The three zero-order associations of occupation, education and owner-
occupancy exhibited significance for at least one definition of delinquency.
In addition, the multiple association of occupancy, occupation and sex of main
wage earner and the partial of owner-occupancy for female wage earners were
significant. However, as in the case of the family structure, no single or set
(at least those tested) of variables was able to account for more than 2 percent
of the variability. In addition, there were no major differences, as measured
by Tau b, between the three definitions of delinquency, and as in the case of
family variables, little seems to be gained by using definitions of delinquency
based upon seriousness of offenses.

To conclude, the socio-economic variables of occupational status, education, home ownership and room density, variables which ecological research has
suggested to be important, have failed to distinguish between the delinquent
and non-delinquent in a high delinquent area.

TABLE 4.12. SUMMARY TABLE FOR ASSOCIATION OF SOCIO-ECONOMIC
VARIABLES AND DELINQUENCY STATUS (AS MEASURED BY
THREE DEFINITIONS OF DELINQUENCY).

		DEFINITION OF DELINQUENCY[1]					
	N	I		II		III	
		Tau b	Chi^2	Tau b	Chi^2	Tau b	Chi^2
TOTAL SAMPLE							
Occup. of Main Wage Earn.	874	.008	7.21^2	.013	11.21^2	.008	7.25^2
Ed. of Main Wage Earn.	853	.011	9.38^2	.004	3.70	.008	6.66^2
Owner-occupancy	918	.005	5.03^4	.002	2.07	.002	1.62
Room Density	921	.002	2.17	.003	2.85	.001	0.55
Occupancy, Sex and Occ. of Main Wage Earner	835	.016	12.99^2	.008	6.55^3	.001	9.04^2
FEMALE MAIN WAGE EARNERS							
Owner-occupancy	313	.014	4.38^4	.013	3.96^4	.009	2.84
MALE MAIN WAGE EARNERS							
Owner-occupancy	522	.001	0.45	<.001	0.05	<.001	<0.01

[1]The three definitions are the same as given in Table 4.1.

[2]Significant at the .01 level.

[3]Significant at the .02 level.

[4]Significant at the .05 level.

[5]Multiple association.

Footnotes:

1. See Albert K. Cohen and James F. Short, Jr., "Juvenile Delinquency" in Robert K. Merton and Robert A. Nisbet (Editors), <u>Contemporary Social Problems</u>, second edition, New York: Harcourt, Brace and World, Inc., 1966, p. 95. And Edwin H. Sutherland and Donald R. Cressey, <u>Principles</u> of <u>Criminology</u>, seventh edition, Philadelphia: J. B. Lippincott Company, 1966, pp. 234-239.
   The principle argument in this area has been over the potential socio-economic biases of official statistics. The issue has already been discussed in Chapter One (See pp. 1-18).

2. Maurice F. Connery, An Ecological Study of <u>Juvenile Delinquency in St. Paul</u>, unpublished Ph.D. dissertation, Columbia University, New York, 1960, p. 58. For details on the occupational scale, see p. 18 in Connery's work.

3. Ronald J. Chilton, <u>Social Factors and the Residential Distribution of Official Delinquents, Indianapolis, Indiana</u>, unpublished Ph.D. dissertation, St. Louis University, St. Louis, 1961, pp. 89-90.

4. Robert H. Hardt and Sandra J. Peterson, "Neighborhood Status and Delinquency Activity as Indexed by Police Records and a Self-Report Survey", unpublished paper presented at the Eastern Sociological Society meetings, Boston, 1964.

5. Tau b = .001, Chi^2 = 1.32, df = 2; .20 $<$ p $<$ .30 (computed by the present author). The occupational classification of 64 boys was not known, leaving a total of 116 youths for this analysis.

6. Albert J. Reiss, Jr. and Albert L. Rhodes, "The Distribution of Juvenile Delinquency in the Social Class Structure", <u>American Sociological Review</u>, 26 (October, 1961), pp. 720-732. The study population consisted of all the white boys, 12 years old and over, who were registered in one of the public, private or parochial junior or senior high schools of Davidson County, Tennessee (N=9,238). Delinquent was any boy adjudged by an official of Davidson County Juvenile Court to be delinquent.
   One major problem in this study is the authors' inconsistent manner of handling offenders whose only offense was a traffic violation. At times in the analysis they are distinguished as a separate category, while at other times they are grouped with delinquents. It is a little difficult to understand why the authors even considered them to be delinquents when almost all other studies have defined them as non-delinquents. Unless otherwise noted, all findings defined traffic offenders as delinquents.

7. Chi^2 = 4.97, df = 2; .02 $<$ p $<$ .05. This considered traffic offenders as non-delinquents. (Tau b and Chi^2 computed by the present author).

8. Defined as containing approximately 75 percent of all students where the head of the household is classified as a blue-collar worker with 50 percent in the lowest of the four major blue-collar occupations.

9. John P. Clark and Eugene P. Wenninger, "Socio-Economic Class and Area as

Correlates of Illegal Behavior among Juveniles", <u>American Sociological Review</u>, 27 (December, 1962), pp. 826-834.

10. The status of the area was measured by occupational distribution.

11. Sheldon Glueck and Eleanor Glueck, <u>Unraveling Juvenile Delinquency</u>, Cambridge, Mass.: Harvard University Press, 1950, p. 99.

12. This particular dividing point was chosen to maximize the association between education and delinquency. For the rationale for this procedure see Robert A. Gordon, "Issues in the Ecological Study of Delinquency", <u>American Sociological Review,</u> 32 (December, 1967), p. 940.

13. See Glenn H. Beyer, <u>Housing: A Factual Analysis</u>, New York: MacMillan Co., 1958, p. 152, and Governor's Advisory Commission on Housing Problems, State of California, <u>Appendix to the Report on Housing in California</u>, April 1963, p. 208.

14. Lillian Cohen, "Family Characteristics of Home Owners", <u>American Journal of Sociology</u>, 55 (May, 1950), p. 566.

15. Bernard Lander, <u>Towards an Understanding of Juvenile Delinquency</u>, New York Columbia University Press, 1954, pp. 55-56.

16. Earl Raab and Gertrude J. Selznick, <u>Major Social Problems</u>, second edition, New York: Harper and Row, 1964, pp. 72-73.

17. H. Ashley Weeks, "Predicting Juvenile Delinquency", <u>American Sociological Review</u>, 8 (February, 1943), p. 41.

18. Published by the Philadelphia Real Estate Directory, Inc., Philadelphia.

19. In many cases the spouse of the owner was the adult respondent. In such cases the deeds were checked (the spouse is almost invariably listed in the deed as co-owner).

20. The Real Estate Directory indicated multiple ownership, but only gave the first appearing name in the deed.

21. See Chapter Two. The 30.5 percent cited above is not quite the proportion of owner-occupied units in the sample because of a few instances of brothe in the sample (who reside in the same unit); although the rate would be very close to 30.5 percent. The figure cited for this sample might be expected to differ from the 1960 census figure because of differences in time and the special nature of the sample; households having 13-15 year-old boys.

22. Underlying this consequence of overcrowding, is the value premise that privacy and solitude are defined as good; to what extent this is always true is a debatable point.

23. Cyril Burt, <u>The Young Delinquent</u>, third edition, London: University of London Press, p. 88.

24. James S. Plant, "Family Living Space and Personality Development", in Norman W. Bell and Ezra F. Vogel (Editors), <u>A Modern Introduction to the Family</u>, Glencoe, Illinois: Free Press, 1960, pp. 510-520.

25. The definition of overcrowding employed for all studies is that of the United States Census, 1.51 persons/room up to 1950 and, in 1960, 1.01/persons/room. In addition to the seven studies listed in Table 4.8, Harlan and Wheery (see Table 4.5) employed three different measures of crowding (all obtained from the United States Census). They are along with the product moment r's with delinquency rates: (1) population/occupied dwelling unit, 0.35; (2) mean number of persons/room, 0.39; (3) percent occupied units with 2.01 persons or more/room, 0.63.

26. <u>Ibid</u>., p. 88.

27. William C. Loring, Jr., "Housing Characteristics and Social Disorganization", <u>Social Problems</u>, 3 (January, 1958), pp. 160-168.

28. Information on number of rooms (which excluded bathrooms) was given by the adult respondent.

29. For a brief discussion of measures of overcrowding, see Alvin L. Schoorr, <u>Slums and Social Insecurity</u>, Washington, D.C.: United States Department of Health, Education and Welfare; Social Security Administration, 1963, p. 17. See the same source, pp. 16-25, for other consequences of overcrowding.

30. The sample was originally divided into sextiles, and the dividing point chosen which maximized the zero-order association between density and delinquency.

31. Herbert J. Gans, <u>The Urban Villagers</u>, New York: Free Press, 1962, pp. 244-246.

32. They were divided into two groups: Skilled, including white-collar, and unskilled, including housewives.

33. These are not directly comparable because of the differences in total N's.

CHAPTER FIVE

INTERPRETATION OF FINDINGS

This study has attempted to discriminate between the delinquent and non-delinquent in a high delinquent area by employing a set of independent variable which for the most part, has been suggested by ecological research to be useful for such a problem. Although a few variables were statistically significant, they contributed little, in terms of variability accounted for, to resolving the problem of this study. There are five possible explanations for these "non-findings":

(1) The methodology used was inadequate, and/or the wrong set of independent variables were used;
(2) delinquency is too complex a phenomenon to be dealt with in this manner;
(3) the assumption of the classic "cause and effect" model is not viable;
(4) area or neighborhood is the major independent variable;
(5) police apprehension less than 100 percent reducing values of statistical association.

Each of these is discussed in turn.

I.   INADEQUATE METHODOLOGY

It is certainly possible that variables not investigated in this study would have proven more successful for the problem at hand. Many other variable often discussed in the literature on delinquency, have been excluded from the present analysis for many reasons. Demographic variables, such as family income and quality of housing, were not included because data was not available. The social psychological variables (e.g., perception of opportunity structures self concept) and personality variables were outside the definition of the problem.

Little can be said about flaws in methodology. Whenever recognized, limitations of method were discussed. However, it is fairly obvious that the researcher is unable to uncover all of his own errors, and it remains for others to provide the necessary critical stance to specify any inadequacies in method.

One major, and potentially serious gap, is the failure to utilize the variable of time. This failure has two important consequences. For one, there is little certainty that the independent variables are in fact antecedent to the acquisition of a J.A.D. record. A few of the variables (e.g., home ownership, altered family) may have been a consequence of having a family member acquire a J.A.D. record rather than the reverse. Thus, it is not always possi to make statements about the direction of cause. Secondly, any interaction between the age of the youth and an independent variable cannot be uncovered. Overcrowding or loss of a parent, for example, may be crucial in the early year of the youth and not when he is in his early teens. Since the data on room density and family structure is only available for the time of the interview, it is impossible to test the interaction of time with overcrowding or altered family.

These are only two variables; the same can be true of many others.

II.   COMPLEXITY

There is general consensus among behavioral scientists that delinquency
is a complex phenomenon. However, it may be even more complex than anyone has
envisioned to date. Complexity is taken to mean the presence of numerous statistical interactions between independent variables so that any zero-order association, or one involving two or three independent variables, accounts for a very
small portion of the total variance of the dependent variable. Delinquency may
involve not only many variables, but a myriad of interactions as well. A few of
the results of this study may point to such an explanation. It may be recalled
that one or two instances of multi-variate analysis produced a larger reduction
of variability than in the case of any one zero-order association. However,
even in these instances no more than 2 to 3 percent of the variability was
accounted for. It might have taken numerous other instances, not tested, to
achieve a moderate degree of success. Unfortunately, there are no statistical
means available to analyze a situation of enormous complexity. The methods
which are available for handling statistical interaction have severe restrictions.
They either are limited to a small number of variables (e.g., analysis of variance), become too cumbersome with a large number of variables (e.g., partial
associations, multiple regression), or require that the interactions be sus-
pected beforehand.[1]   A multi-variate technique is needed which is able to uncover unsuspected interaction for a large number of variables at the same time.[2]

III.   CAUSE AND EFFECT

An implicit, although basic assumption of this study is that the problem
can be analyzed in terms of the classic "cause and effect" model. This model
can be expressed in simple terms: An event B is produced by a prior event A and,
given the same condition, A will always produce B. This approach is a fairly
standard one in delinquency research, and in sociology in general.

> During most of the present century, sociology has devoted its ener-
> gies to the establishment of basic propositions showing that one
> part or aspect of society is related to another part or aspect:
> Religion is related to voting, solidarity is related to suicide,
> education is related to class, delinquency is related to group
> association, and so forth. A basic tool has been some simple sta-
> tistical measure of association showing the relation between two,
> sometimes three variables.[3]

This, of course, is what is implied by the terms independent and dependent
variables. However, to what extent is this assumption viable? Within recent
years in the behavioral sciences, a so-called "systems" approach has been de-
veloping which explicitly contends that the classic "cause and effect" notions
are inadequate for understanding social behavior. The work of Buckley, in perhaps the most recent and comprehensive statement on the systems approach in
sociology, describes it as:

> ......a complex of elements or components directly or indirectly
> related in a causal network, such that each component is related

to at least some others in a more or less stable way within any
particular period of time. The components may be relatively simple
and stable, or complex and changing; they may vary in only one or
two properties or take on many different states. The interrelations
between them may be mutual or undirectional, linear, non-linear or
intermittent, and varying in degrees of causal efficacy or priority.[4]

Buckley speaks about morphogenesis as "those processes which tend to elaborate
or change a system's given form, structure, or state", and "deviation-amplifyi
feed back systems" as one type of morphogenesis.[5] Deviation-amplification whi
is especially germane here, refers to a situation where a slight or small pre
cipitant or event produces a large series of events, through mutual causal lin
within the system, which further move or change the system away from that of t
original condition. The same event under similar conditions may produce dis-
similar results, depending upon the existing and potential feed back networks.

Thomas J. Scheff's[6] theory of mental illness illustrates this deviation-
amplifying process.

> For diverse causes - biological, psychological, and/or social - most
> individuals at some time or other engage in residual rule-breaking
> or unusual behavior that is potentially definable by some members of
> society as abnormal or wrong. Most such residual rule-breaking is
> denied, not defined or reacted to as of consequence, and is thus not
> amplified; it is transitory and without issue. On the other hand,
> depending on the status of the individual, the visibility of his
> residual rule-breaking, community tolerance level, and so on, his
> behavior and its effects on family or friends may lead to a 'public
> crisis' wherein it comes to be defined and 'labeled' as 'mental ill-
> ness'. These social responses of others significant to him, in con-
> junction with his own suggestibility at such a time of stress, and
> along with the stereotyped behaviors of the mentally disturbed he
> has learned during the normal socialization process, all contribute
> to his definition of himself as deviant. Inasmuch as this is un-
> settling to an already disturbed person, his self-control is further
> impared, making further episodes of 'unusual' behavior likely. A
> deviation-amplifying feed back loop is thus set up...reverberating
> from 'ego' and his behavior to significant others, to the public such
> as psychiatrist, court judge, family physician, or solicitous neighbor,
> and back to ego's self-conception. Ego's advance into overt deviant
> role-playing is furthered when the psychiatrist, for example, attempts
> to fit ego's presumed symptoms and verbal responses and punishes him
> for attempting to deny his deviant role. This also constitutes a
> potential deviation-amplifying source, contributing to the final sta-
> bilization of ego into the career deviant role - the neurotic or psy-
> chotic. Finally, the aggregation of such deviant roles has its feed-
> back effects in the community, its structure, its tolerance level, and
> the consequent nature of the 'societal reaction' to further deviance.[7]

In understanding this process, one can basically look at two kinds of variable
They are, (1) those which are responsible for the start of the process, or wha
Lemert calls "original" causes, and those which are internal to the system (e.
in the above illustration, community tolerance level, reaction of friends,
societal reaction), or what Lemert calls "efficient" causes.[8] The important

implication here is that there can be many and diverse original causes, with the consequence that any one original cause will exhibit small, if any, association with the final outcome of deviance.

It is conceivable that the "independent variables" in this study are "original causes", and knowledge of these antecedent events, these supposedly predisposing strain factors, will not help either understand or specify delinquency. Instead, knowledge of the delinquency-producing process, the "efficient causes" (societal reaction, tolerance levels, reaction of officials), would be more useful in accounting for delinquency. This requires knowledge of the "feedback loops", thus making it somewhat meaningless to speak about cause and effect.[9] It is possible that some events have greater probabilities of being "original causes" which may account for the small but significant association on the part of a few of the variables in this study.

IV. AREA AS INDEPENDENT VARIABLE

A third reason which might account for the low association between delinquency rates and the independent variables used in this study is that area or neighborhood may be the major determinant of delinquency. There is some evidence for this view. The studies by Reiss and Rhodes and Clark and Wenninger, previously cited in Chapter Four, have indicated that the occupational status of the area in which the youth resides is more important than the occupation of the youth's father or household head. Shaw argued that factors such as overcrowding and low education were not causal factors in themselves, but indicators of the state of organization within the area. The crucial determinant for delinquency was the area.[10] Thus, in a city-wide study of delinquents, one would find some degree of association between delinquency and such independent variables as quality of housing, overcrowding, home ownership. However, an intensive study of these very same variables within areas would produce little if any association because the area has accounted for most if not all of the variance. (The problem of why not everyone becomes a delinquent in a high delinquency area will be discussed below.) Lander, on the basis of factor analysis, concludes that delinquency is "fundamentally related to the stability or anomie of the area."[11]

A major theoretical approach relevant to the problem of "area" as a determinant, developed within the past twenty years, is the notion of "delinquent subculture". Therefore, it is appropriate that the subcultural theories of delinquency be examined closely.

The term "subculture" has been used with great frequency in the sociological literature (e.g., delinquent subcultures, occupational subcultures, class subcultures, youth subcultures, ethnic subcultures)[12] with little or no attempt despite some obvious conceptual problems, to give the term a fair amount of precision.

The most agreed upon property of the concept is that it postulates a distinctive and unique "style of life" which sets the members of the subculture apart from the "general (larger) culture" of which it is a part. Thus, the crucial elements of the concept are: (1) There are some elements of the subculture which are shared with the general culture, and (2) there are elements which are unique to the subculture and not shared with the larger culture. There are, however, two ways in which this condition can occur.

<u>Type I</u>: A subculture which operates completely within the general culture, maintaining a series of norms and values somewhat distinct from that of the larger culture. These unique constellations of norms and values, at least the important ones of the subculture, are <u>accepted or tolerated</u> by the general society. This is perhaps best illustrated by the so-called occupational subcultures.

<u>Type II</u>: This subculture occurs when the central norms and values that separate the group are, at least in part, <u>not accepted or tolerated</u> by the general culture. These are best illustrated by such conflict groups (for "contra-cultures") as "delinquent subcultures" and certain ethnic groups.

Downes presents a similar classification system based on the origins of the subculture:

(1) Those that precede or are created outside the general culture (e.g., immigrant group);

(2) those that originate within the general culture and represent a "positive response" to that general culture, i.e., the norms and values are accepted by the general culture (e.g., occupation, age group, etc.);

(3) those created within the general culture but constituting a "negative response", i.e., these norms and values are rejected by the general culture.[13]

Although there are certain equivalences between the Downes system and the system presented previously, there are some important differences. First, it is possible for subcultures to precede or originate outside and be in conflict with that of the general culture, (e.g., Japanese Americans in the early 1900's). Thus the Downes Type I could be either Type I or II in the previous system. Secondly, one may be more interested in viewing a subculture at some other time in its life history other than when it was created. It is possible for the value and norms of a subculture to be accepted (or rejected) at the time of its origin and for this view to be reversed at a later time. There are, then, certain purposes for which the Downes system may not prove particularly useful.

One major criticism of the subcultural notion centers on the problem of distinguishing between variation in the general culture and subculture differentiation. Yinger argues that many have taken subculture to be nothing more than role differentiation within a general culture.[14] By this he means that all societies exhibit a range of behavior simply because they permit a large number of roles to exist. Therefore there are differences in norms, values, etc. which are simply attributable to age, sex, occupation, region, etc. To speak about female subcultures or a New England subculture is unnecessary because an acceptable concept, role differentiation, already exists. Perhaps we should reserve the notion of subcultures to a group possessing some semblance of a structure, i.e., interaction and communication between members with recognizable boundaries that demarcate it as a unique group. If we do this, then designations such as "female subculture" are fallacious, since it is extremely doubtful that females constitute a social "group". The more proper concept here for females would be a "social category", a number of persons possessing similar roles (and this can properly be handled under the notion of "role differentiation").[15] Thus, in order to demonstrate the existence of a "subculture", one must determine that <u>both</u>

110

(1) a distinctive style of life exists, and (2) the existence of a group structure. There are, of course, additional problems, particularly as regards the determination of a sufficient condition for a group structure to exist. Since there exists no adequate measuring instruments to ascertain the extent of a structure, it is difficult to determine where a group ends and a non-group begins. The best that one can do at this time is to estimate that one collectivity is more of a group than another collectivity.

Yinger also proposes that a distinction be made between a subculture and "contra-culture".[16] The latter refers to a normative system which contains, "as a primary element, a theme of conflict with the values of the total society". This would be identical with the Type II subculture discussed above. The "subcultural theories" to be discussed below, quite obviously, are examples of "contra-cultures" or Type II subcultures.

In sum, I will take subculture to mean a group which is separated from the rest of society and possesses a portion of its way of life which is common to the rest of society, and a part of its life style as unique. In addition, the subculture should be a collectivity which affects the major portion, if not all, of the life activity of its participants. This qualification is added to preclude certain voluntary organizations (e.g., social clubs and political organizations) from being subsumed under subculture. The subcultures can be of two types: Conflict (or "contra-subculture") or non-conflict, depending on whether the central norms and values of the group are rejected or accepted by the general society. Also of possible relevance is the notion of a "contra-role differentiation", a normative system which is in conflict with the general society, but not necessarily tied to a group but simply to persons occupying the same position (i.e., status) in society).

Subcultural theories of delinquency may be classified as "strain" or "non-strain" theories.[17] The former postulate a factor or number of factors (e.g., anomie, status frustration or deprivation, disorganization, role ambivalence, blocked opportunities, etc.) which predispose youths in the direction of delinquency and are instrumental in producing the "delinquent subculture". In this context the main concern is with the specification of the conditions responsible for the creation of the subculture. The "non-strain" theories view the "delinquent subculture" as an independent variable' the delinquent patterns exist prior to any individual and are learned through a socialization process with no positing of "strain" elements. The "non-strain" theories assume the "delinquent subculture" to exist and are more interested in explaining the persistence rather than the origin.

The most important contemporary exponents of the "strain" theories are Cohen[18] and Cloward and Ohlin.[19] Cohen, by his own admission, does not intend his theory to be a general one of delinquency. His focus is directed upon negative, non-utilitarian, malicious delinquent acts committed by "gangs" of working-class youths. Cohen's theorization of lower-class "gang" delinquency involves "status frustration" as the strain factor. Working class boys have internalized two competing sets of norms and values: The middle-class set (individuality, competitiveness, hard work, economic success goals, respect of property and deferred gratification) obtained through the middle-class institutions (e.g., school, church, mass media),and the working-class set ("good times", importance of friendship, sharing of income, and short-run hedonism). Because of their position in the social structure, the working-class youths perceive that

111

they will be unable to achieve their middle-class aspirations, which in turn produces "status frustration". The youth therefore, turns to the working-clas set of standards, a set which he can more easily adhere to. However, once internalized, the middle-class standards are not easily discarded; they remain i sufficient force to present problems of guilt to the working-class youth. In order to resolve this "psychic" difficulty, the youth, via the mechanism of "reaction-formation", withdraws legitimacy from the middle-class norms by behaving in complete opposition to these norms.[20] This inversion of norms resul in malicious, negativistic and non-ultilitarian acts; acts which have a greate probability of being in violation of the juvenile statutes. This process is carried out by youths who are in communication with others and seek sanction a support, from one another; thus the development of a "delinquent subculture". And according to Cohen, the "delinquent subculture" is a solution to the statu problems of working-class youths.

The "differential opportunity" theory of Cloward and Ohlin is also, by in tention, less than a general theory of delinquency. Their concern is with "ad lescent males in lower-class areas of large urban centers", committing delinqu gang actions. The strain factor they postulate is the discrepancy between aspirations and the legitimate means for achieving these aspirations (i.e., stat frustrations). The youths resolve this "frustrating condition" by withdrawing legitimacy from official norms and opposing them with norms of their own. The resolution is in terms of an utilitarian rationale: the acquisition of the ec nomic success goals by illegitimate, although efficient, means. (This clearly contrasts with Cohen's formulation which involves a repudiation of the success goals and means.) Three hypothetical types of "subcultures" are suggested, ea offering different solutions to status problems. The subcultures are designat as:

(1) Criminal: the concern here is with achievement of material rewards via illegitimate, utilitarian means. This subculture can exist only in areas where there is an already stable, ongoing adult criminal system which provides "illegitimate opportunities" for these youths to later enter the adult criminal world and realize their material aspirations.

(2) Conflict: the principle concern here is for "rep", achieved by acts of violence, force, and threats, which indicate who is the toughest, strongest, and most powerful. Youths are recruited from those who are blocked from the "illegitimate opportunities" as well as the legitimate ones.[21]

(3) Retreatist: this subculture is populated by members who have failed within either the "ciminal" or "conflict" subcultures. Status to them is the achievement of "kicks", "thrills", ecstatic experiences, etc., mainly through the extensive (often addicting) use of drugs, alcohol and sex.

In this model, as with Cohen, the subcultures are solutions to specific status problems generated by structural discontinuities (differential learning struct and opportunity structures). The subcultural norms represent "real answers" to the special problems of lower-class youths, despite the fact that the norms are in conflict with the legal norms of general society.

The most frequently cited example of a "non-strain" theory is that of Walter B. Miller.[22] His major emphasis is on the _entire_ lower class as a way of life rather than a "delinquent subculture" within a larger lower class. Youths residing within lower-class areas are socialized to lower class values involving the "focal" concerns of "trouble", "toughness", "smartness", "excitement", "fate", and "autonomy". Since these concerns and their derivable norms are in conflict with the "law", representing the middle-class values of the society, those who conform to the lower-class values are automatically law-breakers. Consequently, delinquency is viewed as the result of a normal and efficient socialization process, with only those who successfully internalize the lower-class code being more prone to delinquency. Miller, as with the two previous subcultural theories, also sees delinquency as a response to status problems. However, unlike the previous subcultural theorists the achievement of status for lower-class youths is gained simply by adherence to the dictates of the lower-class culture, and not to a variant form of that culture (i.e., "delinquent subculture"). The implication of Miller's position is that delinquency is the consequence of _external_ conflict, where only one value system is internalized. Cohen and Cloward and Ohlin tend to see a conflict between two value systems which are simultaneously internalized.

One of the major issues concerns the interpretation of the term "gang" delinquency within the various theories discussed. Both Cohen and Cloward and Ohlin refer to "gang delinquency" which _might_ imply the presence of a highly complex structure (i.e., explicit division of labor, formalized relationships between roles, explicit group boundaries recognized by both members and outsiders). If this is the case, then their theories are quite clearly subcultural, since the term "gang" meets the prerequisites for a subculture described above. However, some have questioned the validity and usefulness of "gang delinquency". Jackson Toby has argued that a small (less than 10%) proportion of Juvenile Court cases in the United States can be characterized as "gang delinquencies".[23] Yablonsky has questioned the existence of a "gang" and sees them as amphorous collectivities with no clear cut boundries, division of labor, etc. (a "near-group").[24] It seems upon inspection, however, that the notion of "gang" may be unnecessary to the major formulations of Cohen and Cloward and Ohlin. Their theories seem to apply to an informal group; a more amphorous, loosely structured collectivity. To what extent they are still justified in speaking about "delinquent subcultures", remains debatable.

The "delinquent subculture" is often assumed to be less relevant to the formulations of Miller. His emphasis is on the lower class "way of life", rather than a "delinquent subculture" within the lower class; and this seems to involve an even more amphorous collectivity than Cohen and Cloward and Ohlin imply. Downes believes that Miller's approach encompasses a wider range of delinquency, so that even the "stable corner boy" may commit a large number of delinquent acts.[25] This implies therefore, that the demands on the two approaches are different. Cohen and Cloward and Ohlin must explain why some lower-class boys are _not_ influenced by the "delinquent subculture". For Miller, there is no variance to explain since all lower-class youths are potential delinquents. However, Miller still faces the problem of accounting for lower-class boys who do not become "official delinquents". If Miller is interpreted correctly, there seem to be only two solutions he may offer for this problem. Either external factors, such as police activity, varying ability to avoid apprehension, etc., are operating; or not all lower-class youths fully internalize the lower-class value system. If Miller chooses the latter explanation, then he must specify the conditions which account for differential socialization, which, in effect, places him close to the "strain" theories.

Miller, may in fact be in agreement with the "strain" notions if another paper, not often cited, is indicative of his position. In this later paper he views the lower class as a three-fold division; the "stable lower class", the "aspiring but conflicted lower class", and the "successfully aspiring lower class".[26] The second category is very similar to the dimensions that Cohen Cloward and Ohlin speak about:

> ....those for whom familh or other community influences have pro-
> duced a desire to elevate their status, but who lack the necessary
> personal attributes or cultural 'equipment' to make the grade, or
> for whom cultural pressures effectively inhibit aspirations.[27]

It is fairly clear that the "aspire-conflict" response for Miller is the releva one for delinquency with the other two responses being of less consquence.

> "Many of those lower-class youngsters who are in the 'stable'
> group and even some who are upwardly mobile to a slight degree...
> can manage to live out their adolescence as relatively law-
> abiding youngsters who get into little serious trouble with the
> law."[28]

The implication therefore is that Miller is not too far from using a "delinque subculture" model.

Although the major concern of these approaches is different (origin vs. transmission), each theorist makes statements about the others' problem. Mill fleetingly and superficially suggests that the "female dominant household" and "masculine role ambiguities" may be factors in the creation of the peculiar "f concerns" of the lower class.[29] Cohen argues that the problem of persistence of the "delinquent subculture" is independent of the conditions responsible fo its creation. He seems to imply that any single person may or may not have th status problems resulting in the origin of the "delinquent subculture", but he may still be attracted to it (for whatever reason) and subsequently become a delinquent.

> Once such a sub-culture is established, however, its ability to
> contribute to the solution of....other problems may well tip the
> balance in favor of participation for this individual or that.[30]

It certainly seems plausible that the conditions responsible for the orig of a subculture are not necessarily those important for the persistence of the subculture. It is quite conceivable that once a "delinquent subculture" is formed, it acquires a logic, a force or inertia of its own and it is therefore in a sense, a "cause" of delinquency.

Despite the fact that Miller may not be an example of a "non-strain" theo the problem of whether or not "delinquent subculture" is an independent or de-pendent variable is still a valid one. Assuming that a "delinquent subculture" already exists, can it act as a cause of individual delinquency independent of any general and common "strain" factors? Or are there variables ("broken home absence of male role model, overcrowding, etc.) which push individuals into delinquency and a "delinquent subculture" simultaneously or cause them to "join" the subculture and subsequently become delinquents?

If the "delinquent subculture" is an independent variable the issue of why all lower-class youths are not influenced by the subculture (i.e., become delinquent) must still be faced. The available evidence indicates that the vast bulk of youths do eventually become official delinquents. Kobrin, on a re-analysis of data from Chicago, states that two-thirds of the boys from high delinquent areas have delinquent records by the time they pass the age of juvenile status.[31] Savitz, in a more careful analysis of migrant and non-migrant Negro males, concludes that 59 percent of the youths who have resided in the study neighborhood (high delinquent) the "full eleven years of delinquency risk have acquired delinquency records by the time they are 18."[32] This all tends to support the notion of subculture as an independent variable. However, there are, according to previous estimates, still 33-40 percent of the youths who are not delinquent. In the present study approximately 65 percent do not have J.A.D. records. Is it still possible to adhere to the subcultural notion in the light of this seemingly contradictory evidence? One possible conclusion is to assume that some youths who have committed delinquency offenses escape detection by the officials. If this is true, then the seemingly low delinquency rates of the present sample can be explained by a time variable. It is fairly obvious that the probability of being classified a delinquent is a cumulative one.[33] Therefore the older one becomes the greater the probability of being influenced by the delinquent subculture and of being apprehended at least once. Thus, the delinquency rates for the youths in the present sample should be much higher by the time they reach the legal status of adult, since the average age of boys is about 15 and they face three more years of exposure to delinquency and possible apprehension. It still is conceivable that some will still, even after that time, have avoided apprehension.

There is another possibility, which still allows for the validity of "delinquent subculture" as an independent variable, why all lower-class youths do not become delinquent. The area, for both this study and the theories cited above, are large; and it is conceivable that these subcultural forces are not of equal strength throughout the lower-class areas.

> One explanation of the presence of non-delinquents in areas of high
> delinquency is the limitation on contact with delinquency patterns,
> even in the most delinquent areas. A delinquency area is practically
> never solidly delinquent; rather, there are certain streets or parts
> of streets on which at a particular time most delinquents reside, and
> on other streets the children may associate with each other in relative
> isolation from the behavior pattern of delinquents.[34]

(This notion of a geographic discontinuity of "delinquent subcultural" forces undercuts the notion that the general lower class culture is directly responsible for delinquency.) One interesting implication of this last possibility is that delinquency may be, in part, a chance event; it may simply be a matter of being in a certain place for a certain length of time.

To conclude, the subcultural notions have argued that certain areas in our large cities have value and normative systems which are, in one manner or another, related to delinquency. However unlike the explicit arguments of the "strain" theorists, the "delinquent subculture" may be more important in accounting for individual delinquency, rather than a small set of factors pushing individuals into the "delinquent subcultures". Such variables as broken homes, overcrowded households, homeownership may simply be indicators, or even causes, of the "delinquent subculture", but they have little relevance for individuals becoming delinquents in high delinquent areas. If this is true, then the importance of ecological research, as a legitimate approach to understanding delinquency, is enhanced.

The systems approach as outlined in a previous section, is compatible with the subcultural explanation. Individuals may be attracted to the "delinquent subculture" for diverse reasons ("original causes") but once attracted, they are molded by the subculture ("efficient causes") into delinquency. The process of becoming a delinquent via the delinquent subculture could, therefore, involve the hardware of the systems approach (e.g., feedback loops).

V. APPREHENSION RATES

The final explanation for the lack of strong findings involves the probability of apprehension. It is fairly obvious that not all youths who commit potentially definable delinquent acts are known to the J.A.D. There are, therefore, some youths who could be considered in some "real" sense delinquents who never acquire a J.A.D. record. What proportion of youths in a high delinquent area could be classified as "undetected delinquents" is not known. (Some youths who have never committed a delinquent act still acquire a J.A.D. record, if they are apprehended by the J.A.D who suspect them of delinquency. It would seem, however, that the proportion of falsely accused would be less than the undetected; how much less there is no way of knowing from the present data. It will be assumed in the following discussion that a very small number of boys with J.A.D. records have not committed delinquencies.) Although the evidence is meager, there are some who feel that the values of high delinquency area would result in a lowering of the apprehension rate. For example, Sellin and Wolfgang argue that:

> ...in some delinquency areas where subcultural values are hostile
> to law enforcement generally, many victims prefer to settle matters
> informally rather than by contacting the police or they may refuse
> to prosecute or bear witness if theoffense is reported. A minor
> fight or theft, which most certainly would be reported in some dis-
> tricts, is considered too common an occurrence in high delinquency
> areas to bring to the attention of the police.[35]

Some supporting evidence for this view is found in the findings of a recent survey of citizen cooperation with police in high crime areas in Boston and Chicago. Reiss concludes, "that there is considerable crime where the citizen is a victim and yet they say they did not report it to the police".[36] There were two paramount reasons given for the non-reporting: (1) the police could do little to apprehend the offender, and (2) too troublesome (takes too much time or the possibility of getting "involved" in court proceedings.) Reiss speculates that the greater the cost of the crime to the victim the greater the chance of notifying the police.

> ...there does seem to be reason to believe that citizens do not
> call the police unless they regard a matter as something where

they were seriously wronged or they are personally affronted, or where they have something personally to gain from it, such as gain from an insurance claim. But any gain has to be worth the effort of calling the police and "getting involved". Apart from such motivations to call the police citizens are inclined to disengage themselves from any responsibility to call the police.[37]

Demonstrating the existence of a probability of apprehension to be less than one is insufficient for present purposes. The important question still remains: What effect does this have on the measured association between recorded delinquency and a set of independent variables? In an attempt to answer the question, the following hypothetical situation is proposed. If we assume that the actual rate of delinquency is 50 percent (i.e., the proportion of youths who have committed at least one delinquent act, not necessarily known to the J.A.D.) and an independent variable X was a necessary and sufficient condition of delinquency, then the 2 x 2 table for a sample of 100 youths and 50-50 split in the row marginals would be the following:

	Del.	Non-Del	
X	50	0	50
Non-X	0	50	50
	50	50	100

The Tau b for such a table would be 1.000. If the probability of apprehension was independent of X and 0.30, then only 15 of the actual delinquents would now be listed as official delinquents (J.A.D. record). The 2 x 2 table would now be:

	J.A.D.	Non-J.A.D.	
X	15	35	50
Non-X	0	50	50
	15	85	100

Here the observed Tau b is reduced to .176, a reduction of approximately 72 percent. This is, of course, only one specific example for one set of conditions. Would the result be the same for differing probabilities of apprehension and values of "true associations"? A similar analysis was conducted for several selected values of apprehension probabilities and "true associations"; the results of which are given in Table 5.1. As can easily be seen, the Tau b's are reduced for all levels of apprehension probabilities, no matter what the value of the "true association". However, the rate of reduction is not the same for all values of "true association". If one were to graph (apprehension probability by observed Tau b) the results of Table 5.1, one could easily see that the rate of reduction of the observed Tau b values, produced by decreasing apprehension probabilities, is more rapid the higher the value of the "true association". In addition, the difference in rates of reduction between the various "true associations" curves is the greatest at the upper range of the apprehension probabilities.

TABLE 5.1.   OBSERVED TAU b VALUES FOR ASSOCIATION
OF X AND MEASURED DELINQUENCY (J.A.D.
RECORD) FOR SELECTED LEVELS OF TRUE
ASSOCIATION AND PROBABILITY OF APPRE-
HENSION.

TRUE ASSOCIATION (Tau b)	PROBABILITY OF APPREHENSION			
	0.10	0.30	0.50	0.80
1.00	.053	.176	.333	.798
0.85	.053	.163	.282	.540
0.64	.053	.107	.200	.429
0.36	.019	.077	.120	.240
0.16	.009	.030	.051	.107
0.04	.003	.007	.013	.027

This is not a systematic analysis of the problem, and the results in Table 5.1
are for the constant conditions of a 50 percent rate of "actual delinquency"
and a 50-50 split in the row marginals. A change in these conditions might produce a different set of results, although it is fairly obvious that a reduction
in the degree of association would still occur. The only intent of this crude
and ad hoc analysis was to demonstrate that a less than 100 percent apprehension
rate will reduce the degree of association between an independent variable and
delinquency.

One possible way to circumvent the contaminating factor of apprehension rate
would be to deal with unofficial delinquents, that is use self-reports as the
measure of delinquency. However, if the self-report instrument showed every
youth to have committed at least one delinquent act, then there would be no variance to explain, and the apprehension issue would be inconsequential (although
if a sub-cultural notion was relevant, then, as discussed above, apprehension
rates would be of consequence). If such a situation occurred, then the self-
report measures would have to be divided into the most delinquent and the least
delinquent, as most self-report studies do. The usual dimensions employed in
self-report instruments to produce such a dichotomy are frequency of delinquent
acts and seriousness of the act. If this be the case, and if the self-reports
are to be considered alternatives to official delinquency in this context, then
one has to assume that seriousness and frequency do not increase the probability
of apprehension. Otherwise, official delinquency would reflect the same dichot-
of most delinquent and least delinquent that the self-reporting instruments
are supposedly measuring, and nothing would be gained by the use of self-report
measures (i.e., both instruments would measure the same thing). Here again, the
issue of apprehension rates would be inconsequential. If the self-report studi
produce low associations between delinquency and the same or similar independer
variables employed in this study, then the issue of apprehension rates would n
be a factor in explaining the small associations utilizing official records as

118

the measure of delinquency. This conclusion is warranted, of course, only if the self-report instruments prove to be valid. To the extent to which this study has examined the findings of self-report studies, there is little reliable evidence to indicate that they would produce a different set of results than utilizing official delinquency records.

One final issue seems of importance, namely why ecological correlations reviewed in this study are almost invariably higher than individual correlations found in the present study for the same or similar variables?[38]

One possible reason is suggested by Robinson and is primarily a function of the mathematical properties of ecological correlation.[39] Ecological correlations (r_e) are functions of the total individual correlation (r) and the within-area correlations (r_w). When $r_w < r$, then $r_e > r$. Since r_w is almost always less than r, because of the increased homogeneity of the population within areas,[40] then the ecological correlations are almost always larger than the total individual correlations.

A second possible explanation involves the issue of apprehension rates. Their contaminating effects, as discussed above, can be minimized in ecological correlations if the effect of apprehension rates is constant over areas.[41] This, of course, is only true if the independent variables exhibited variance over areas. When contaminating effects of the apprehension rates are removed, the ecological correlations would naturally show higher values over correlations for individuals.

Finally, if area is the important determinant for delinquency, one would also expect higher ecological associations. Such conditions as low home ownership and high overcrowding could produce an area which is crimogenic in nature, and youths residing in such areas would have a greater chance of becoming delinquent, independent of whether they possessed the same characteristics which were responsible for producing the crimogenic area.

In summary, the family and socio-economic factors investigated in this study has contributed very little to the understanding and specification of individual delinquency in a high delinquent area. Several possible explanations have been suggested for these "non-findings", however, without further evidence, there was no basis for deciding which of the five alternatives discussed is critical. The resolution of this dilemma must await further research.

Footnotes:

1. For an example of this method, see Hubert M. Blalock, "Theory Building and
   the Statistical Concept of Interaction", _American Sociological Review_, 30
   (June, 1965), pp. 374-380.

2. A technique is available which meets these requirements: _Predictive Attri-
   bute Analysis_, which is comprehensively described in P.MacNaughton-Smith,
   Some Statistical and Other Numerical Techniques for Classifying Individuals,
   London, Her Majesty's Stationary Office, 1965. The technique is illustrated
   in Lawrence Rosen and Stanley H. Turner, "An Evaluation of the Lander Approach
   to Ecology of Delinquency", _Social Problems_, 15 (Fall, 1967), pp. 189-200.
   MacNaughton-Smith (p. 21) states that in situations where all the zero-order
   associations are small, the technique will produce a very low yield. Thus
   the fact that no single zero-order association was more than .015 (Tau b)
   in the present study argued against the use of the technique.

3. Walter Buckley, _Sociology and Modern Systems Theory_, Englewood Cliffs, New
   Jersey: Prentice-Hall, 1967, p. 66. This is similar to Matza's evaluation
   of a good portion of contemporary work in delinquency. See David Matza,
   Delinquency and Drift, New York: John Wiley and Sons, 1964, Chapter One.

4. Buckley, _op_. _cit_., p. 41.

5. _Ibid_., p. 58.

6. Cited in Buckley, _op_. _cit_., p. 169.

7. _Ibid_., pp. 170-171.

8. Edwin M. Lemert, _Social Pathology_, New York: McGraw-Hill Company, 1951,
   pp. 75-76.

9. A similar, but more systematic treatment of deviance can be found in Leslie
   T. Wilkins, _Social Deviance_, Englewood Cliffs, New Jersey: Prentice-Hall
   1965.

10. Clifford R. Shaw, _et al_., _Delinquency Areas: A Study of the Geographic Dis-
    tribution of School Truants, Juvenile Delinquents and Adult Offenders in
    Chicago_, Chicago; University of Chicago Press, 1929, p. 205.

11. Bernard Lander, _Towards an Understanding of Juvenile Delinquency_, New York
    Columbia University Press, 1954, p. 59. Robert A. Gordon, "Issues in the
    Ecological Study of Delinquency", _American Sociological Review_, 32 (December
    1967), pp. 927-944, in a recent critique of current ecological research of
    delinquency, has seriously questioned Lander's conclusion. After a thorough
    and devastating evaluation of Lander's statistical methodology Gordon con-
    cludes that Lander's evidence conclusively points only to a strong socio-
    economic interpretation of delinquency and not an "anomic" one. Also
    questioning Lander's assertion although from a less substantial base than
    Gordon's, is Rosen and Turner, _op_. _cit_., pp. 192-193.

12. For example, in a widely used introductory text book, the authors speak
    about ethnic, regional, occupational and student subcultures. See Leonard

Broom and Philip Selznick, _Sociology_, Third Edition, New York: Harper and Row, 1963, pp. 60-61, 452-456.

13. David M. Downes, _The Delinquent Solution: A Study in Subcultural Theory_, London: Routledge and Kegan Paul, 1966, p. 9.

14. J. Milton Yinger, "Contraculture and Subculture", _American Sociological Review_, 25 (August, 1960), pp. 625-635.

15. It is conceivable that role differentiation may be of a conflict nature (values and norms not accepted by the "general culture") or a non-conflict nature (values and norms accepted by the general culture).

16. Yinger, _op. cit._

17. These are sometimes referred to in the literature as "anomic" and "cultural transmission" theories, respectively.

18. Albert K. Cohen, _Delinquent Boys: The Culture of the Gang_, Glencoe, Illinois: The Free Press, 1955.

19. Richard A. Gloward and Lloyd E. Ohlin, _Delinquency and Opportunity: A Theory of Delinquent Gangs_, New York: The Free Press, 1960.

20. Cohen has been criticized widely for his incorporation of Freud's concept of "reactionformation". (For example of such a criticism, see J. I. Kitsuse and D. C. Dietrick, "Delinquent Boys: A Critique", _American Sociological Review_, 24 (1959), pp. 208-215.) In fact, he himself has conceded and indicated that "reaction formation" is not a necessary facet of the theory. See Downes, _op. cit._, p. 44 where reference is made to this point in an unpublished paper by Cohen.

21. This response is very similar to Cohen's malicious, negativistic non-utilitarian youths.

22. Walter B. Miller, "Lower Class Culture as a Generating Milieu of Gang Delinquency", _Journal of Social Issues_, 14 (Number 3, 1958), pp. 5-19.

23. Jackson Toby, "Delinquency and Opportunity: A Critique", _British Journal of Sociology_, 12 (December, 1961), pp. 282-289.

24. Lewis Yablonsky, "The Delinquent Gang as a Near Group", _Social Problems_, 7 (Fall, 1959), pp. 108-117.

25. Downes, _op. cit._, p. 72.

26. William C. Kvaraceus and Walter B. Miller, "Norm-Violating Behavior and Lower Class Culture" in Ruth Shonle Cavan (Editor), _Readings in Juvenile Delinquency_, Philadelphia: J. B. Lippincott Company, 1964, pp. 56-66. (Reprinted from their _Delinquent Behavior, Culture and the Individual_, Washington D.C.: National Education Association of the United States, 1959.)

27. _Ibid._, p. 64. These terms are similar to other similar classifications: White's "stable corner boy" and "college boy"; Gans' "routine seekers" and

"action seekers"; S. M. Miller and Reisman's "irregular worker" and "stable worker".

28. _Ibid._, p. 66.

29. Miller (1958), _op. cit._

30. Cohen, _op. cit._, p. 153.

31. Solomon Kobrin, "The Conflict of Values in Delinquency Areas", _American Sociological Review_, 16 (October, 1951), pp. 653-661.

32. Leonard Savitz, "Delinquency and Migration", in Marvin Wolfgang, L. Savitz and W.Johnson (Editors), _The Sociology of Crime and Delinquency_, New York: John Wiley and Sons, 1962, p. 205. The measurement of delinquency was Juvenile Court appearance, the use of a J.A.D. record may have produced a much higher figure. (See Chapter One, in the present study.)

33. John C. Ball, Alan Ross and Alice Simpson, "Incidence and Estimated Prevalence of Recorded Delinquency in a Metropolitan Area", _American Sociological Review_, 29 (February, 1964), pp. 90-93, and Alan Little, "The Prevalence of Recorded Delinquency and Recidivism in England and Wales", _American Sociological Review_, 30 (April, 1965), pp. 260-63.

34. Edwin H. Sutherland and Donald R. Cressey, _Principles of Criminology_, Seventh Edition, Philadelphia: J. B. Lippincott, 1966, pp. 197-198.

35. Thorsten Sellin and Marvin E. Wolfgang, _The Measurement of Delinquency_, New York: John Wiley and Sons, 1964, p. 107.

36. Albert J. Reiss, Jr., _Public Perceptions and Recollections About Crime, Law Enforcement, and Criminal Justice_, unpublished monograph, Survey Research Center, University of Michigan, 1967, p. 67.

37. _Ibid._, p. 69.

38. W. S. Robinson, "Ecological Correlations and the Behavior of Individuals", _American Sociological Review_, 15 (June, 1950), pp. 351-357, reports that ecological variables are almost invariably higher than correlations for individuals.

39. _Ibid._

40. The more restricted the range of the variable, the more likely the value of product moment r would be smaller.

41. I am grateful to Stanley H. Turner for suggesting this point.

MAP OF STUDY AREA

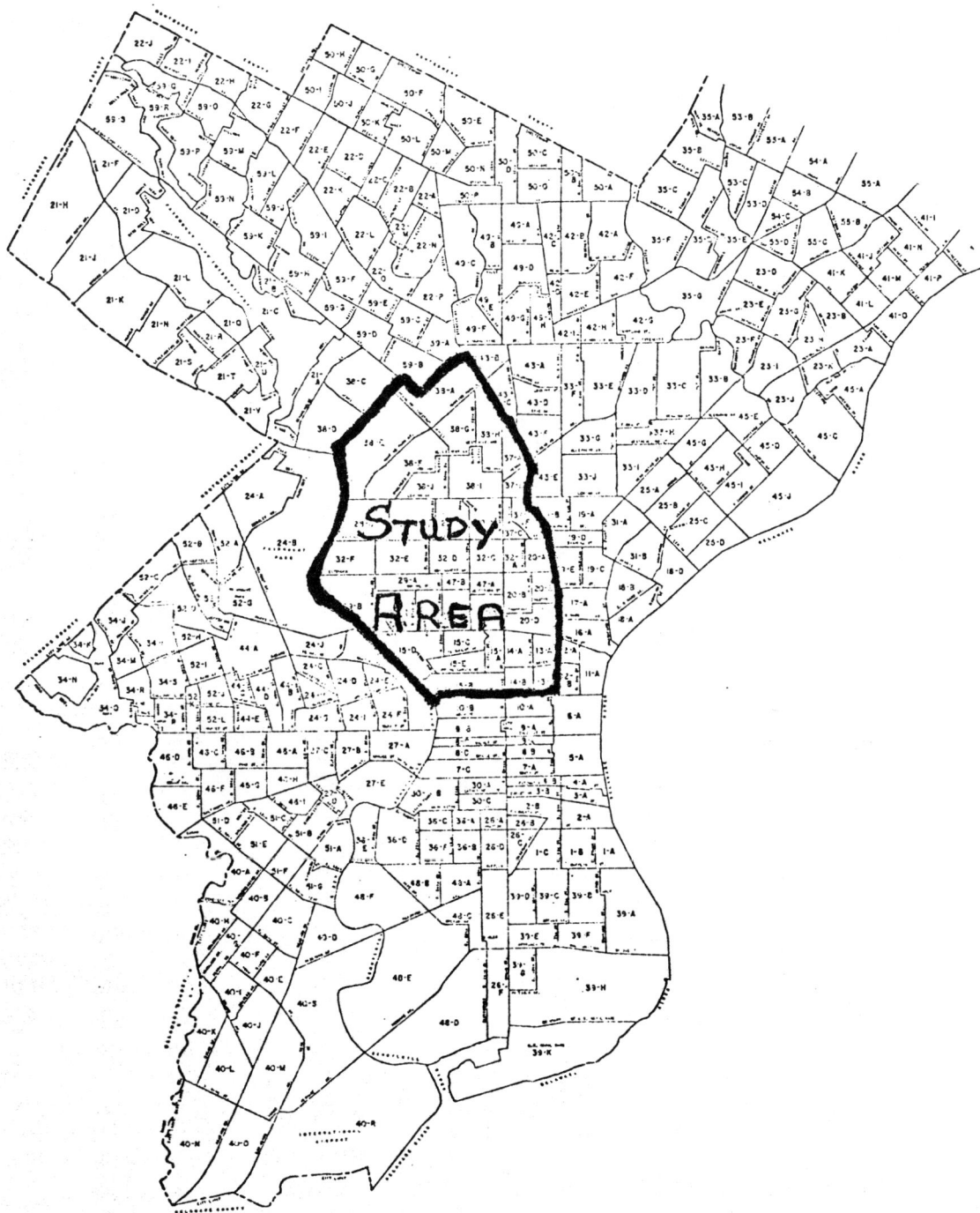

1960
PHILADELPHIA CENSUS TRACTS

Sampling Procedure

The geographic universe of the study (see map on page 123) was the area bounded by Roosevelt Expressway and Roberts Avenue on the north, Germantown Avenue and Sixth Street on the east, Vine Street on the south, and on the west by the Schuylkill River. The area includes all of the following 41 1960 census tracts:

13 A, B;
14 A, B:
15 A, B, C, D, E;
20 A, B, D, E;
28 A, B, C, D;
29 A, B, C, D;
32 A, C, D, E, F;
37 A, B, C, F;
38 A, E, F, G, H, I, J;
47 A, B, C, D.

The sampling procedure employed was "area probability" (a type of cluster sample). Three hundred blocks (as defined by the 1960 census) were randomly selected and each of the blocks sub-divided into "land segments" (resulting in a total of 1200 segments), with each "segment" containing an average of forty occupied dwelling units. A total of 887[1] "segments" were selected and every household in the segment canvassed. A total of approximately 30,000 households were covered from June 17 to August 30, 1963 to determine if an "eligible" youth was present. An eligible youth was defined as a male born on or between July 1, 1948 and June 30, 1950 (i.e., 13-15 year old males). By this process a total of 1017 youths were selected as eligible and a total of 997 interviewed (a completion rate of 98 percent). In addition to these "area sample" youths, two other sources of eligible youths were incorporated. These were all youths attending Glen Mills and Daniel Boone Schools[1] as of June 1963 and who listed their place of residence in the study area. This added sample increased the total number of youths to 1098, representing 1023 households. An influential adult[2] was interviewed for each youth, resulting in 1069[1] joint interview (one youth and one adult) and 29 single interviews (youth only). All sampling and interviewing were completed by National Analysts, Inc., Philadelphia, Pennsylvania.

For purposes of this study, several cases were eliminated for various reasons:

Reason	Number
Whites	136
No identifiable surname	4
Duplicate interviews	8
No adult interview	21
Adult not living in household	1
Address given outside of the study area	2
Unable to locate deed of the dwelling unit	5
Total	177

Thus the total sample utilized for this study was 921, representing 861 households.

[1]The number of segments chosen was governed by the goal of acquiring approximately 1000 eligible youths.

[1]These are "special schools" for youths in Philadelphia. Glen Mills is an institution for "delinquents" involving institutionalization of the youth. It is privately owned, state aided, and for boys 8-16 with I.Q.'s above 70. One must be assigned there from the Juvenile Court. The Boone School is under the jurisdiction of the Philadelphia Board of Education and is designed to handle special discipline problems. Youths assigned to this school live at home and do not necessarily possess a J.A.D. record. There are two major points that should be considered as a result of this added sample of youths. For one, this insured that all eligible boys who live in the canvassed households and who were residing at Glen Mills at the time of the study would be included in the sample. However, this does not exhaust all sources of institutionalization, either for delinquency, hospitalization, etc. Evidence is lacking concerning the possible error that this would produce; however, one should allow for the possible under-reporting of an institutionalized population. In addition, the inclusion of the added sample introduces non-random considerations. This means that one cannot utilize the total sample for purposes of population estimation. If one wants some statement about population parameters, then one must consult the original 997 "area sample" youths. Perhaps the major concern here is that the delinquency rate and the proportion of institutionalized delinquents might both be over-stated.

[2]The influential adult was defined as the one whom the youth designated in answering the question, "Who in your family influences you the most". If the person named was a male, he was interviewed. If the adult was a female, then the second most influential was chosen only if he were a male. The aim was to maximize the number of male adult respondents.

[1]The overall completion rate for the matched interviews was 97.5 percent (1069 out of 1098). However, there was a large difference in completion rates between the "area sample" and the "institutional sample" with the rate of the former being 99.4 percent and the latter 77.0 percent. Since those youths not having adult interviews are discarded for this study, one must keep in mind the potential bias introduced of eliminating a proportionately larger segment of the institutionalized population.

TABLE 1.   JUVENILE DELINQUENCY STATUS (AS MEASURED BY
           PRESENCE OF JUVENILE AID DIVISION RECORD AND
           THE MOST SERIOUS OFFENSE ON THE RECORD) BY
           PRESENCE OR ABSENCE OF PARENTS.

	MOST SERIOUS OFFENSE IN J.A.D. RECORD.				NO RECORD	TOTAL
	PERSON[1]	PROPERTY[2]	JUV. STATUS[3]	OTHER[4]		
BOTH PRESENT	34	70	38	39	341	522
FATHER ABSENT	28	47	22	24	147	268
MOTHER ABSENT	5	3	0	2	10	20
BOTH ABSENT	3	11	5	5	32	56
DISAGREE*	3	8	7	3	34	55
TOTAL	73	139	72	73	564	921

[1] Person offenses: rape, robbery, assault and battery (aggravated and non-aggravated).

[2] Property offenses: burglary, larceny, malicious mischief.

[3] Juvenile status offenses: runaway, truancy, curfew.

[4] Other offenses: weapons, sex (non-commercial), disorderly conduct.

*Cases where there was disagreement between adult and youth on the presence of parents.

TABLE 2. JUVENILE DELINQUENCY STATUS (AS MEASURED BY
PRESENCE OF JUVENILE AID DIVISION RECORD AND
THE MOST SERIOUS OFFENSE ON THE RECORD) BY
STATUS OF ABSENT PARENT.

	MOST SERIOUS OFFENSE IN J.A.D. RECORD				NO RECORD	TOTAL
	PERSON	PROPERTY	JUV. STATUS	OTHER		
BOTH PARENTS PRESENT	34	70	38	39	341	521
FATHER ALIVE	21	33	15	17	104	190
FATHER DEAD	7	12	5	6	31	61
MOTHER ALIVE	3	0	0	3	6	12
MOTHER DEAD	2	2	1	1	2	8
ONE PARENT DEAD, ONE PARENT ALIVE	0	2	0	0	8	10
BOTH PARENTS ABSENT AND ALIVE	1	8	4	3	13	29
BOTH PARENTS DEAD	0	0	0	0	7	7
UNKNOWN	3	5	3	1	20	32
DISAGREE*	2	7	6	3	33	51
TOTAL	73	139	72	73	564	921

*Cases where there was disagreement between adult and youth on the presence of parents. There are four less disagreements here than in Table 1 because four of the "disagrees" in Table 1 were coded as unknown for the analysis in this table.

TABLE 3.   JUVENILE DELINQUENCY STATUS (AS MEASURED BY
PRESENCE OF JUVENILE AID DIVISION RECORD AND
THE MOST SERIOUS OFFENSE ON THE RECORD) BY
PRESENCE OF ADULT MALES (OVER EIGHTEEN YEARS
OF AGE) IN HOUSEHOLD OF YOUTH.

MOST SERIOUS OFFENSE IN JAD RECORD

	PERSON	PROPERTY	JUV. STATUS	OTHER	NO RECORD	TOTAL
FATHER PRESENT	39	74	38	41	350	542
FATHER ABSENT--OTHER ADULT MALE PRESENT	5	20	8	3	41	77
NO ADULT MALE PRESENT	21	34	19	26	130	230
DISAGREE*	8	11	7	3	43	72
TOTAL	73	139	72	73	564	921

*Cases where there was disagreement between adult and youth on the presence
of parents or other adult males when father was absent.

TABLE 4.   JUVENILE DELINQUENCY STATUS (AS MEASURED BY PRESENCE
OF JUVENILE AID DIVISION RECORD AND THE MOST SERIOUS
OFFENSE ON THE RECORD) BY SEX OF HOUSEHOLD HEAD.

MOST SERIOUS OFFENSE IN J.A.D. RECORD

	PERSON	PROPERTY	JUV. STATUS	OTHER	NO RECORD	TOTAL
MALE	46	87	42	44	387	606
FEMALE	23	47	23	26	138	257
DISAGREE*	4	5	7	3	36	55
UNKNOWN	0	0	0	0	3	3
TOTAL	73	139	72	73	564	921

*Cases where there was disagreement between adult and youth on the presence
of parents. (Since the father was defined as head of household when present it
could not be determined who was the head for the disagreements.)

TABLE 5.   JUVENILE DELINQUENCY STATUS (AS MEASURED BY PRESENCE
OF JUVENILE AID DIVISION RECORD AND THE MOST SERIOUS
OFFENSE ON THE RECORD) BY SEX OF MAIN WAGE EARNER.

MOST SERIOUS OFFENSE IN J.A.D. RECORD

	PERSON	PROPERTY	JUV. STATUS	OTHER	NO RECORD	TOTAL
MALE	45	77	36	44	376	578
FEMALE	22	54	29	24	153	282
BOTH	0	0	0	0	2	2
UNKNOWN	6	8	7	5	33	59
TOTAL	73	139	72	73	564	921

TABLE 6.   JUVENILE DELINQUENCY STATUS (AS MEASURED BY PRESENCE
OF JUVENILE AID DIVISION RECORD AND THE MOST SERIOUS
OFFENSE ON THE RECORD) BY SEX OF MAIN DECISION MAKER.

MOST SERIOUS OFFENSE IN J.A.D. RECORD

	PERSON	PROPERTY	JUV. STATUS	OTHER	NO RECORD	TOTAL
MALE	26	40	19	25	213	323
FEMALE	45	92	52	47	335	571
ENTIRE FAMILY	0	0	0	0	1	1
BOTH PARENTS	0	0	0	0	2	2
UNKNOWN	2	7	1	1	13	24
TOTAL	73	139	72	73	564	921

TABLE 7.   JUVENILE DELINQUENCY STATUS (AS MEASURED BY
           PRESENCE OF JUVENILE AID DIVISION RECORD AND
           THE MOST SERIOUS OFFENSE ON THE RECORD) BY
           SEX OF ADULT LIVING IN HOUSEHOLD WHO INFLU-
           ENCES THE YOUTH MOST.

MOST SERIOUS OFFENSE IN J.A.D. RECORD

	PERSON	PROPERTY	JUV. STATUS	OTHER	NO RECORD	TOTAL
MALE	13	32	20	25	143	233
FEMALE	60	107	52	47	416	682
BOTH	0	0	0	0	1	1
UNKNOWN	0	0	0	1	4	5
TOTAL	73	139	72	73	564	921

TABLE 8. JUVENILE DELINQUENCY STATUS (AS MEASURED BY PRESENCE OF JUVENILE AID DIVISION RECORD AND THE MOST SERIOUS OFFENSE ON THE RECORD) BY SEX OF DECISION MAKER PARTIALED FOR FAMILY STRUCTURE (PRESENCE OR ABSENCE OF PARENTS).*

MOST SERIOUS OFFENSE IN J.A.D. RECORD

	PERSON	PROPERTY	JUV. STATUS	OTHER	NO RECORD	TOTAL
BOTH PARENTS PRESENT						
MALE	20	32	14	23	186	275
FEMALE	13	33	23	16	148	233
UNKNOWN	1	5	1	0	7	14
FATHER ABSENT						
MALE	2	2	2	0	9	15
FEMALE	26	43	20	23	134	246
UNKNOWN	0	2	0	1	4	7
MALE	3	2	0	1	7	13
FEMALE	2	1	0	1	3	7
UNKNOWN	0	0	0	0	0	0
MOTHER ABSENT						
MALE	3	2	0	1	7	13
FEMALE	2	1	0	1	3	7
UNKNOWN	0	0	0	0	0	0
MALE	3	2	1	0	5	11
FEMALE	3	8	4	5	24	44
UNKNOWN	0	0	0	0	1	1

*Excludes 55 cases where there was disagreement between adult and youth on the presence of parents.

TABLE 9. JUVENILE DELINQUENCY STATUS (AS MEASURED BY PRESENCE OF
JUVENILE AID DIVISION RECORD AND THE MOST SERIOUS OFFENSE
ON THE RECORD) AND SEX OF ADULT WHO INFLUENCES THE YOUTH
MOST PARTIALED FOR FAMILY STRUCTURE (PRESENCE OR ABSENCE
OF PARENTS).*

MOST SERIOUS OFFENSE IN J.A.D. RECORD

	PERSON	PROPERTY	JUV. STATUS	OTHER	NO RECORD	TOTAL
			BOTH PARENTS PRESENT			
MALE	9	25	17	22	128	201
FEMALE	25	45	21	16	211	318
UNKNOWN AND BOTH	0	0	1	0	2	3
			FATHER ABSENT			
MALE	0	1	2	0	3	6
FEMALE	28	46	20	24	141	259
UNKNOWN	0	0	0	0	3	3
			MOTHER ABSENT			
MALE	3	2	0	1	7	13
FEMALE	2	1	0	1	3	7
UNKNOWN	0	0	0	0	0	0
			BOTH PARENTS ABSENT			
MALE	1	3	0	1	4	9
FEMALE	2	8	5	4	28	47
UNKNOWN	0	0	0	0	0	0

*Excludes 55 cases where there was disagreement between adult and
youth on the presence of parents.

TABLE 10.   JUVENILE DELINQUENCY STATUS (AS MEASURED BY PRESENCE OF
JUVENILE AID DIVISION RECORD AND THE MOST SERIOUS OFFENSE
ON THE RECORD) BY SEX OF HOUSEHOLD HEAD PARTIALED FOR
FAMILY STRUCTURE (PRESENCE OR ABSENCE OF PARENTS).*

MOST SERIOUS OFFENSE IN J.A.D. RECORD

	PERSON	PROPERTY	JUV. STATUS	OTHER	NO RECORD	TOTAL
BOTH PARENTS PRESENT						
MALE	34	70	38	39	341	522
FEMALE	0	0	0	0	0	0
UNKNOWN	0	0	0	0	0	0
FATHER ABSENT						
MALE	4	4	2	1	18	29
FEMALE	22	43	20	23	128	236
UNKNOWN	2	0	0	0	1	3
MOTHER ABSENT						
MALE	5	3	0	2	10	20
FEMALE	0	0	0	0	0	0
UNKNOWN	0	0	0	0	0	0
BOTH PARENTS ABSENT						
MALE	3	7	2	2	18	32
FEMALE	0	4	3	3	10	20
UNKNOWN	0	0	0	0	4	4

*Excludes 55 cases where there was disagreement between adult and
youth on the presence of parents.

TABLE 11. JUVENILE DELINQUENCY STATUS (AS MEASURED BY PRESENCE OF JUVENILE
AID DIVISION RECORD AND THE MOST SERIOUS OFFENSE ON THE RECORD)
BY SEX OF MAIN WAGE EARNER PARTIALED FOR FAMILY STRUCTURE (PRESENCE
OF PARENTS).*

MOST SERIOUS OFFENSE IN J.A.D. RECORD

	PERSON	PROPERTY	JUV. STATUS	OTHER	NO RECORD	TOTAL
			BOTH PARENTS PRESENT			
MALE	31	61	27	37	318	474
FEMALE	1	5	5	0	15	26
UNKNOWN AND						
BOTH	2	4	6	2	6	20
			FATHER ABSENT			
MALE	5	5	1	2	13	26
FEMALE	19	39	20	20	118	216
UNKNOWN	4	3	1	2	16	26
			MOTHER ABSENT			
MALE	5	3	0	2	9	19
FEMALE	0	0	0	0	0	0
UNKNOWN	0	0	0	0	1	1
			BOTH PARENTS ABSENT			
MALE	3	5	3	0	15	26
FEMALE	0	5	2	4	11	22
UNKNOWN	0	0	0	0	4	4

*Excludes 55 cases where there was disagreement between adult and
youth on the presence of parents.

TABLE 12. JUVENILE DELINQUENCY STATUS (AS MEASURED BY PRESENCE OF JUVENILE
AID DIVISION RECORD AND THE MOST SERIOUS OFFENSE ON THE RECORD) BY
ORDINAL POSITION OF YOUTH.

MOST SERIOUS OFFENSE IN J.A.D. RECORD

	PERSON	PROPERTY	JUV. STATUS	OTHER	NO RECORD	TOTAL
OLDEST	17	34	17	20	181	269
INTERMEDIATE	36	67	35	27	215	380
YOUNGEST	11	20	11	13	92	147
ONLY	8	16	8	13	73	118
UNKNOWN	1	2	1	0	3	7
TOTAL	73	139	72	73	564	921

TABLE 13. JUVENILE DELINQUENCY STATUS (AS MEASURED BY PRESENCE OF
JUVENILE AID DIVISION RECORD AND THE MOST SERIOUS OFFENSE
ON THE RECORD) BY ORDINAL POSITION OF YOUTH PARTIALED FOR
FAMILY STRUCTURE (PRESENCE OR ABSENCE OF PARENTS).*

MOST SERIOUS OFFENSE IN J.A.D. RECORD

	PERSON	PROPERTY	JUV. STATUS	OTHER	NO RECORD	TOTAL
BOTH PARENTS PRESENT						
ELDEST	11	18	13	11	113	166
INTERMEDIATE	18	41	19	12	137	227
YOUNGEST	4	8	5	9	57	83
ONLY	1	2	1	7	32	43
UNKNOWN	0	1	0	0	2	3
FATHER ABSENT						
ELDEST	4	10	3	5	50	72
INTERMEDIATE	14	22	11	12	57	116
YOUNGEST	5	8	2	4	21	40
ONLY	4	7	5	3	18	37
UNKNOWN	1	0	1	0	1	3
MOTHER ABSENT						
ELDEST	0	2	0	1	1	4
INTERMEDIATE	2	1	0	1	4	8
YOUNGEST	1	0	0	0	2	3
ONLY	2	0	0	0	3	5
UNKNOWN	0	0	0	0	0	0
BOTH PARENTS ABSENT						
ELDEST	0	1	1	1	8	11
INTERMEDIATE	2	1	0	1	6	10
YOUNGEST	0	1	2	0	4	7
ONLY	1	7	2	3	14	27
UNKNOWN	0	1	0	0	0	1

*Excludes 55 cases where there was disagreement between adult and
youth on the presence of parents.

TABLE 14. JUVENILE DELINQUENCY STATUS (AS MEASURED BY PRESENCE OF JUVENILE AID DIVISION RECORD AND MOST SERIOUS OFFENSE ON RECORD) BY HOUSEHOLD SIZE (NUMBER OF PERSONS).

MOST SERIOUS OFFENSE IN J.A.D. RECORD.

	PERSON	PROPERTY	JUV. STATUS	OTHER	NO RECORD	TOTAL
TO TO SIX	40	79	37	38	362	566
SEVEN TO FIFTEEN	33	60	35	25	202	355
TOTAL	73	139	72	73	564	921

TABLE 15. JUVENILE DELINQUENCY STATUS (AS MEASURED BY PRESENCE OF JUVENILE AID DIVISION RECORD AND MOST SERIOUS OFFENSE ON RECORD) BY FAMILY STRUCTURE (PRESENCE OR ABSENCE OF PARENTS) PARTIALED FOR HOUSEHOLD SIZE (NUMBER OF PERSONS).*

MOST SERIOUS OFFENSE ON J.A.D. RECORD.

	PERSON	PROPERTY	JUV. STATUS	OTHER	NO RECORD	TOTAL
SMALL (2 - 6 PERSONS)						
BOTH PARENTS PRESENT	19	26	15	24	203	287
FATHER ABSENT	14	38	13	19	108	192
MOTHER ABSENT	4	3	0	1	5	13
BOTH PARENTS ABSENT	1	7	4	2	26	40
LARGE (7 - 15 PERSONS)						
BOTH PARENTS PRESENT	15	44	23	15	138	235
FATHER ABSENT	14	9	9	5	39	76
MOTHER ABSENT	1	0	0	1	5	7
BOTH PARENTS ABSENT	2	4	1	3	6	16

*Excludes 55 cases where there was disagreement between adult and youth on the presence of parents.

TABLE 16. JUVENILE DELINQUENCY STATUS (AS MEASURED BY PRESENCE
OF JUVENILE AID DIVISION RECORD AND THE MOST SERIOUS
OFFENSE ON THE RECORD) BY OCCUPATION OF MAIN WAGE
EARNER IN HOUSEHOLD.

MOST SERIOUS OFFENSE IN J.A.D. RECORD

	PERSON	PROPERTY	JUV. STATUS	OTHER	NO RECORD	TOTAL
SKILLED AND WHITE COLLAR	19	37	25	29	223	333
UNSKILLED	27	71	30	24	214	366
HOUSEWIFE	20	26	13	17	99	175
UNKNOWN	7	5	4	3	28	47
TOTAL	73	139	72	73	564	921

TABLE 17. JUVENILE DELINQUENCY STATUS (AS MEASURED BY PRESENCE
OF JUVENILE AID DIVISION RECORD AND THE MOST SERIOUS
OFFENSE ON THE RECORD) BY YEARS OF EDUCATION COMPLETED
FOR MAIN WAGE EARNER IN HOUSEHOLD.

MOST SERIOUS OFFENSE IN J.A.D. RECORD

	PERSON	PROPERTY	JUV. STATUS	OTHER	NO RECORD	TOTAL
LOW (0 - 9 YEARS)	36	72	37	40	233	418
HIGH (10 - 16 YEARS)	28	60	30	30	287	435
UNKNOWN	9	7	3	5	44	68
TOTAL	73	139	72	73	564	921

TABLE 18.   JUVENILE DELINQUENCY STATUS (AS MEASURED BY PRESENCE OF JUVENILE
            AID DIVISION RECORD AND THE MOST SERIOUS OFFENSE ON THE RECORD) BY
            OCCUPANCY STATUS OF DWELLING UNIT OF YOUTH'S HOUSEHOLD.

MOST SERIOUS OFFENSE IN J.A.D. RECORD

	PERSON	PROPERTY	JUV. STATUS	OTHER	NO RECORD	TOTAL
OWNER-OCCUPIED	19	36	15	24	187	281
NON-OWNER-OCCUPIED	54	103	57	49	374	637
UNKNOWN	0	0	0	0	3	3
TOTAL	73	139	72	73	564	921

TABLE 19.   JUVENILE DELINQUENCY STATUS (AS MEASURED BY PRESENCE OF JUVENILE
            AID DIVISION RECORD AND THE MOST SERIOUS OFFENSE ON THE RECORD) BY
            SEX AND OCCUPATION OF MAIN WAGE EARNER AND TENURE OF DWELLING UNIT
            OF YOUTH'S HOUSEHOLD.

MOST SERIOUS OFFENSE IN J.A.D. RECORD

	PERSON	PROPERTY	JUV. STATUS	OTHER	NO RECORD	TOTAL
MALE, SKILL., OWN.	9	12	2	12	81	116
MALE, SKILL, NON-OWN.	7	13	13	10	89	132
FEMALE, SKILL, OWN.	1	1	2	2	13	19
FEMALE, SKILL, NON-OWN.	2	9	4	3	32	50
MALE, UNSKILL., OWN.	6	17	7	6	62	98
MALE, UNSKILL., NON-OWN.	15	31	12	10	108	176
FEMALE, UNSKILL., OWN.	1	2	0	2	15	20
FEMALE, UNSKILL., NON-OWN.	23	42	21	22	116	224
UNKNOWNS	9	12	11	6	48	86
TOTAL	73	139	72	73	564	921

TABLE 20. JUVENILE DELINQUENCY STATUS (AS MEASURED BY PRESENCE OF
JUVENILE AID DIVISION RECORD AND THE MOST SERIOUS OFFENSE
ON THE RECORD) BY ROOM DENSITY (PERSONS PER ROOM).

MOST SERIOUS OFFENSE IN J.A.D. RECORD

	PERSON	PROPERTY	JUV. STATUS	OTHER	NO RECORD	TOTAL
0.20 - 0.62	11	20	12	17	103	163
0.64 - 0.80	11	20	8	12	99	150
0.82 - 0.91	8	18	10	11	64	111
1.00 - 1.12	8	25	13	9	99	154
1.14 - 1.33	19	23	17	14	106	179
1.38 - 4.00	16	33	12	10	93	164
TOTAL	73	139	72	73	564	921

Andry, Robert G., "Faulty Paternal and Maternal-Child Relationships, Affection and Delinquency", _British Journal of Delinquency_, 8 (July, 1959), pp. 34-38.

Ball, John C., Alan Ross and Alice Simpson, "Incidence and Estimated Prevalence of Recorded Delinquency in a Metropolitan Area", _American Sociological Review_, 29 (February, 1964), pp. 90-93.

Barker, Gordon H., "Family Factors in the Ecology of Juvenile Delinquency", _Journal of Criminal Law and Criminology_, 30 (January-February, 1940), pp. 681-691.

Bates, William Mary, _The Ecology of Juvenile Delinquency in St. Louis_, unpublished Ph.D. dissertation, Washington University, 1959.

_____, "Caste, Class and Vandalism", _Social Problems_, 9 (Spring, 1962) pp. 349-353.

Bell, Robert R., "The One-Parent Family: A Conceptual View", unpublished paper, 1965.

Bordua, David J., "Juvenile Delinquency and Anomie", _Social Problems_, 6 (Winter, 1958), pp. 230-238.

Bossard, James H. S., _Parent and Child_, Philadelphia: University of Pennsylvania Press, 1953.

Bowlby, John, _Maternal Care and Mental Health_, Geneva: World Health Organization 1952.

Browning, Charles J., "Differential Impact of Family Disorganization on Male Adolescents", _Social Problems_, 8 (Summer, 1960), pp. 37-44.

Buckley, Walter, _Sociology and Modern Systems Theory_, Englewood Cliffs, New Jersey: Prentice-Hall, 1967.

Burt, Cyril, _The Young Delinquent_, third edition, London: University of London Press, 1938.

Carr-Saunders, A. M., Hermann Mannheim and E. C. Rhodes, _Young Offenders_, New York: MacMillan, 1944.

Chilton, Ronald Judson, _Social Factors and the Residential Distribution of Official Delinquents, Indianapolis, Indiana_, unpublished Ph.D. dissertation Indiana University, 1962.

_____. "Continuities in Delinquency Area Research", _American Sociological Review_, 29 (February, 1964), pp. 71-83.

Clark, John P. and Eugene P. Wenninger, "Socio-Economic Class and Area as Correlates of Illegal Behavior among Juveniles", _American Sociological_

Review, 27 (December, 1962), pp. 826-834.

Cloward, Richard A. and Lloyd E. Ohlin, _Delinquency and Opportunity: A Theory of Delinquent Gangs_, New York: Free Press of Glencoe, 1960.

Cohen, Albert K., _Delinquent Boys: The Culture of the Gang_, Glencoe, Illinois: Free Press of Glencoe, 1955.

Conlin, James J., _An Area Study of Juvenile Delinquency in Baltimore_, Maryland, unpublished Ph.D. dissertation, St. Louis University, 1961.

Cohen, Lillian, "Family Characteristics of Home Owners", _American Journal of Sociology_, 55 (May, 1950), pp. 565-571.

Connery, Maurice F., _An Ecological Study of Juvenile Delinquency in St. Paul_, unpublished Ph.D. dissertation, Columbia University, 1960.

Costner, Herbert L., "Criteria for Measures of Association", _American Sociological Review_, 30, (June, 1965), pp. 341-353.

Downes, David M., _The Delinquent Solution: A Study in Subcultural Theory_, London: Routledge and Kegan Paul, 1966.

Glueck, Sheldon and Eleanor Glueck, _Unraveling Juvenile Delinquency_, New York: Commonwealth Fund, 1950.

Goodman, Leo A. and William H. Kruskal, "Measures of Association for Cross Classification", _Journal of the American Statistical Association_, 49 (December, 1954), pp. 732-764.

Gordon, Robert A., "Issues in the Ecological Study of Delinquency", _American Sociological Review_, 32 (December, 1967), pp. 927-944.

Hardt, Robert H. and Sandra J. Peterson, "Neighborhood Status and Delinquency Activity as Indexed by Police Records and a Self-Report Survey", unpublished paper presented at Eastern Sociological Society Meetings, Boston, 1964.

_____, "Delinquency and Social Class: Studies of Juvenile Deviations or Police Disposition?" unpublished paper presented at Eastern Sociological Society Meetings, New York, 1965.

_____.and George E. Bodine, _Development of Self-Reporting Instruments in Delinquency Research_, Syracuse, New York: Syracuse University Youth Development Center, 1965.

_____.and Sandra J. Peterson, "How Valid are Self-Report Measures of Delinquent Behavior", unpublished paper presented at Eastern Sociological Society Meetings, Philadelphia, 1966.

Harlan, Howard and Jack Wherry, "Delinquency and Housing", _Social Forces_, 27 (October, 1948), pp. 58-61.

Kobrin, Solomon, "The Conflict of Values in Delinquency Areas", _American_

        Sociological Review, 16 (October, 1951), pp. 653-661.

Kvaraceus, William C. and Walter B. Miller, "Norm-Violating Behavior and Lower
        Class Culture", in Ruth Shonle Cavan (Editor), _Readings in Juvenile_
        Delinquency, Philadelphia: J. B. Lippincott, 1964, pp. 56-66. (Re-
        printed from their _Delinquent Behavior, Culture and the Individual_,
        Washington, D. C.: National Education Association of the United
        States, 1959.)

Lander, Bernard, _Towards an Understanding of Juvenile Delinquency_, New York:
        Columbia University Press, 1954.

Lees, J. P. and L. J. Newsom, "Family or Sibship Position and Some Aspects of
        Juvenile Delinquency", _British Journal of Delinquency_, 5 (July, 1954),
        pp. 46-65.

Lemert, Edwin M., _Social Pathology_, New York: McGraw-Hill, 1951.

Little, Alan, "The 'Prevalence' of Recorded Delinquency and Recidivism in Eng-
        land and Wales", _American Sociological Review_, 30 (April, 1965),
        pp. 260-263.

Loring, William C., Jr., "Housing Characteristics and Social Disorganization",
        Social Problems, 3 (January, 1956), pp. 160-168.

McCord, Joan and William McCord, "The Effects of Parental Role Model in Crimi-
        nality", in Ruth Shonle Cavan (Editor), _Readings in Juvenile Delin-_
        quency, Philadelphia: J. B. Lippincott, 1964, pp. 170-180.

McEachern, A. W. and Riva Bauzer, "Factors Related to Disposition in Juvenile
        Police Contacts", in Malcolm W. Klein (Editor), _Juvenile Gangs in_
        Context, Englewood Cliffs, New Jersey: Prentice-Hall, 1967, pp. 148-16

Mannheim, Hermann, _Comparative Criminology_, Boston: Houghton Mifflin, 1965.

Matza, David, _Delinquency and Drift_, New York: John Wiley and Sons, 1964.

Miller, Walter B., "Lower Class Culture as a Generating Milieu of Gang Delin-
        quency", _Journal of Social Issues_, 14 (Number 3, 1958), pp. 5-19.

Ness, Siri, "Mother-Child Separation and Delinquency", _British Journal of De-_
        linquency, 10 (July, 1959), pp. 22-33.

Nye, F. Ivan, _Family Relationships and Delinquent Behavior_, New York: John
        Wiley and Sons, 1958.

Parsons, Talcott, "The Social Structure of the Family", in Ruth Nanda Anshen
        (Editor), _The Family: Its Function and Destiny_, revised edition,
        New York: Harper and Brothers, 1959, pp. 257-258.

Peterson, Donald R. and Wesley C. Becker, "Family Interaction and Delinquency",
        in Herbert C. Quay, (Editor), _Juvenile Delinquency_, Princeton, New
        Jersey: D. Van Nostrand, 1965, pp. 63-99.

Plant, James S., "Family Living Space and Personality Development", in Norman
    W. Bell and Ezra F. Vogel (Editors), A Modern Introduction to the
    Family, Glencoe, Illinois: Free Press, 1960, pp. 510-520. (Reprinted
    from James S. Plant, Personality and the Cultural Pattern, Cambridge,
    Massachusetts: Harvard University Press, 1937, pp. 213-218.

Rainwater, Lee, "Crucible of Identity: The Negro Lower-Class Family", in
    Talcott Parsons and Kenneth B. Clark (Editors), The Negro American,
    Boston: Houghton Mifflin, 1966, pp. 160-204.

Reckless, Walter C., Simon Dinitz and Ellen Murray, "Self Concept as an Insulator
    against Delinquency", American Sociological Review, 21 (December, 1956),
    pp. 744-746.

Reiss, Albert J., Jr., and Albert Lewis Rhodes, "The Distribution of Juvenile
    Delinquency in the Social Class Structure", American Sociological
    Review, 26 (October, 1961), pp. 720-732.

Robinson, W. S., "Ecological Correlations and the Behavior of Individuals",
    American Sociological Review, 15 (June, 1950), pp. 351-357.

Rodman, Hyman and Paul Grams, "Juvenile Delinquency and the Family: A Review
    and Discussion", unpublished paper prepared for the President's
    Commission on Law Enforcement and Administration of Justice, 1967.

Rosen, Lawrence and Stanley H. Turner, "An Evaluation of the Lander Approach
    to Ecology of Delinquency", Social Problems, 15 (Fall, 1967), pp. 189-
    200.

Savitz, Leonard, "Delinquency and Migration", in Marvin E. Wolfgang, Leonard
    Savitz and Norman Johnston (Editors), The Sociology of Crime and Delin-
    quency, New York: John Wiley and Sons, 1962, pp. 199-205.

Scarpitti, Frank, et al., "The 'Good' Boy in a High Delinquency Area; Four
    Years Later", American Sociological Review, 25 (August, 1960), pp. 555-
    558.

Schorr, Alvin L., Slums and Social Insecurity, Washington, D. C.: United States
    Department of Health, Education and Welfare, Social Security Administra-
    tion, 1963.

Sellin, Thorsten and Marvin E. Wolfgang, The Measurement of Delinquency, New
    York: John Wiley and Sons, Inc., 1964.

Shaw, Clifford, et al., Delinquency Areas, Chicago: University of Chicago Press,
    1929.

_____, and Henry D. McKay, "Are Broken Homes a Causative Factor in Juvenile
    Delinquency", Social Forces, 10 (May, 1932), pp. 415-515.

_____, and Henry D. McKay, Juvenile Delinquency and Urban Areas, Chicago:
    University of Chicago Press, 1942.

Sletto, Raymond, "Sibling Position and Juvenile Delinquency", American Journal of Sociology, 39 (March, 1934).

Sterne, Richard S., Delinquent Conduct and Broken Homes, New Haven: College and University Press, 1964.

Sutherland, Edwin H. and Donald R. Cressey, Principles of Criminology, seventh edition, Philadelphia: J. B. Lippincott, 1966.

Tangri, Sandra S. and Michael Schwartz, "Delinquency Research and the Self-Concept Variable", The Journal of Criminal Law, Criminology and Police Science, 58 (October, 1967), pp. 182-190.

Tennyson, Ray A., "Family Structure and Delinquent Behavior", in Malcolm W. Klei (Editor), Juvenile Gangs in Context, Englewood Cliffs, New Jersey: Prentice-Hall, 1967, pp. 57-69.

Toby, Jackson, "The Differential Impact of Family Disorganization", American Sociological Review, 22 (October, 1967), pp. 502-512.

_____, "Delinquency and Opportunity: A Critique", British Journal of Sociology, 12 (December, 1961), pp. 282-289.

Weeks, H. Ashley and Margaret G. Smith, "Juvenile Delinquency and Broken Homes in Spokane, Washington", Social Forces, 18 (October, 1939), pp. 48-55.

_____, "Male and Female Broken Home Rates by Type of Delinquency", American Sociological Review, 5 (August, 1940), pp. 601-609.

_____, "Predicting Juvenile Delinquency", American Sociological Review, 8 (February, 1943), pp. 40-46.

Wilkins, Leslie T., "Juvenile Delinquency: A Critical Review of Research and Theory", Educational Research, 5 (February, 1963), pp. 104-119.

_____, Social Deviance, Englewood Cliffs, New Jersey: Prentice-Hall, 1965.

Yablonsky, Lewis, "The Delinquent Gang as a Near Group", Social Problems, 7 (Fall, 1959), pp. 108-117.

Yinger, J. Milton, "Contraculture and Subculture", American Sociological Review, 25 (August, 1964), pp. 625-635.